the
Resume | Cover Letter | Portfolio | Handbook
THE COMPREHENSIVE GUIDE FOR COLLEGE STUDENTS AND JOB SEEKERS

John DiMarco, Ph.D.

CONTRIBUTIONS BY KASEY WAGNER,
GRACE BRASKY, AND SAMANTHA CHENG

independently published by
Portfoliovillage, Inc.
www.portfoliovillage.com

PORTFOLIOVILLAGE

Dedications

For my loving family, Kim, David, and Jack. You are everything.

For my students, who keep me passionate
about teaching and learning.

Acknowledgments

Sincere thanks to the incredible communication
professionals who worked with me on this book.
Kasey Wagner
Samantha Cheng
Grace Brasky
I'm grateful for your skills, talent, and dedication
to helping me with my own creativity.

Thank you to my **St. John's University family** of colleagues.
My faithful academic home for the last two decades.

Book design and typography by
John DiMarco and Samantha Cheng.

Contents

INTRODUCTION
Happiness is the goal.

What you will learn
- How to assess your own career happiness (ch 1)
- How to measure compensation against happiness (ch 2)
- How to research jobs and analyze skills and keywords (ch 3)
- How to write and design an intelligence resume (ch 4)
- How to write and edit a persuasive cover letter (ch 5)
- How to plan and layout a print and PDF portfolio book (ch 6)
- How to plan and build an effective web portfolio (ch 7)

Why you may be worried about making your resume
I understand the fear and anxiety you may have when thinking about making your resume, cover letter and portfolio. This occurs because the process and your own abilities present unknowns. My expertise as an educator is to help you overcome those unknowns by guiding you in gaining knowledge and skills, and to give you the tools you need to be confident.

You will be a stronger candidate for any job if you follow my proven process and techniques. I know how effective these techniques are because I've seen the results. I realize the responsibility I have as an educator to provide the most valuable information and useful techniques to help you reach your goals – so I truly care about your learning and success.

You get full support like no other book on the market. I provide the ultimate career education experience. You get access to **Step by step instructions** on writing and design supported by a **library of template files** in our PortfolioVillage learning center, which includes quality tested resume files, cover letter files, professional portfolio book files, and online web portfolio site templates.

I'll transfer confidence to you by helping you create a resume that yields call backs and email responses requesting interviews. Then I'll teach you how to make a professional portfolio, regardless of your major, that helps you land the freelance gig, internship, or the job. I've been doing this consistently for 25 years – helping students, new graduates, and young professionals figure out how to connect their happiness with their careers.

What you will create

- resume
- cover letter
- reference sheet

- Web portfolio
- print portfolio book (PDF)

Downloadable templates are included for resume, cover letter, print portfolio, web portfolio and reference sheet.

Plus,
- Includes career research and branding exercises
- Full color examples of career documents
- Step by Step learning examples to teach you quickly
- Based on science behind resume content & design
- Free limited access to the PortfolioVillage Learning Center

Getting started

1. Go to www.portfoliovillage.com and set up your free account.
2. Once you have your account, download the template documents to your computer (resume, cover letter, reference sheet, and portfolio books)
3. Read each chapter of this book, take notes in the text, and use the templates to create the documents. You can refer to the text and free video lessons and lectures at www.portfoliovillage.com.
4. Access the Google sites reference materials at portfoliovillage.com to create your web portfolio.

Scan to access portfoliovillage.com for templates, video lectures from Dr. DiMarco and step by step lessons.

I wish you the best in your learning journey and quest for finding happiness.
Dr. John DiMarco
Professor of Communication and Design
St. John's University
New York City

Chapter 1.

HAPPINESS
Identify what you want in a job.

Chapter objectives
- Build your confidence
- Identify current career happiness requirements
- Define happiness elements in a job or industry
- Identify and understand what makes you happy right now

Welcome
Although it's common to jump into any job straight out of college or high school, it's important to know the difference between what you want and what you don't want in a job. When you take a job that you are not truly interested in, going to work becomes more like a chore.

The key to knowing what you want is to perform research, which you learn about in the next chapters. Job and industry research are vital to understanding what you may want in a career. It also allows you to highlight what you may want to avoid.

In this book, you'll use research to seek out what will make you happy in your job and career.

Then you'll learn how to create career communication in the form of a resume, cover letter, and portfolio.

You'll use these career tools to secure jobs that make you happy across multiple touch points.

But for now, you need to know what you are shopping for in a job, the touch points that contribute to your happiness, comfort, and self-actualization.

Job touch points
All jobs provide different points that connect the organization and the individual to create a bond of happiness. These points include the tangible things that a company offers such as recurring money, health benefits, and merchandise discounts. Touch points can also include the intangible things like pride in

the company mission and one's work. These items all add to a level of happiness for you, so you need to understand what they are and ask some simple questions in your mind when making a plan to find jobs that can yield happiness in your life.

The work

It's best to understand the work that you will be performing before jumping into a job. Is the work going to engage your interests, creativity, and current skills?

If you are not passionate about the workload, it may result in dissatisfaction with your job. When job searching, pay close attention to what the position entails and make sure that it's something you can see yourself doing for hours and possibly years to come.

ASK YOURSELF
Will it propel you to gain skills and experience that can then be applied to your next position?

The company

Before applying to a job or accepting an offer, research must be conducted in order to know about the company and if it fits your happiness needs. The more you know about how it fits your happiness criteria and if you are a possible fit, the more likely you are to want the job and get it. If you have what the employer is looking for, and you want to do those tasks and projects, it becomes a much better "match".

Researching a company is not only the best way to stand out, but it also helps you know if that is the right place. Conducting company research can help you find out what the company does and what they're looking for in a candidate. Important things to know about a company are the company's culture, mission and values, the skills they value – then you show them that you have those qualities in your resume and portfolio.

Maybe you want to work in non-profit because you believe in helping people or a cause. You will want to learn as much as you can about what it is like working for non-profit organizations, what they do, how they impact society, and what you might do working for them. Are they a service business or do they sell products? These questions will help you understand the role of the company in society.

ASK YOURSELF
What are the mission and methods of this company and do I find them interesting to be engaged and growing.?

Salary

Salary is an important part of accepting a job offer. It is the amount that a person is getting paid in money, not benefits, for a specific position. Salaries can be a fixed payment that are typically paid on a monthly or biweekly basis. Or, you may be paid as a freelancer, making an hourly rate. A person's salary typically fluctuates with age as one gains experience.

Higher salaries can lead to job satisfaction, but it is important to remember that a person should pursue a career that gives them personal happiness in addition to a good salary. Remember to figure out how much you will need to live before accepting a salary. You'll learn more about this in the next chapter.

ASK YOURSELF
How much money do I need to live a healthy, happy life (be reasonable)?

Benefits

Many employers will offer benefits as part of a position. The "benefits package" consists of extra perks and compensation offered to employees. This is in addition to the employer's salary.

Types of benefits include main compensation items such as retirement accounts, health insurance, dental insurance, life insurance, paid time off, bonuses, and other sideline items such as company product discounts and tickets to sports and entertainment events. Maybe even a company car, or cell phone.

While it is not necessary to turn down a job offer if all of these benefits aren't presented, they may become more and more valuable as your career extends or your needs grow. Think about how important health insurance is if you or someone in your family gets sick. Or, how important retirement savings will be when you are older.

ASK YOURSELF
How valuable could a company product discount, health insurance, retirement savings, or a no cost car be to your monthly expenses?

Growth

Career growth and development can be the top item you may look for in a job. It's important to invest your time in companies that allow employees to grow in the workplace. With growth, comes the feeling of getting better at something and developing as a professional. Finding a work environment that encourages growth, development, and promotion is important when looking for a job.

ASK YOURSELF
Is there a path for growth into new roles and advancement in the organization I am interested in working with?

Recognition

Recognition in the workplace is a great way to boost an employee's confidence and make them feel more appreciated by others. When a company recognizes an employee, they are acknowledging their performance at work. The goal is to reinforce positive behaviors, practices, or activities that will result in satisfaction and motivation to maintain or improve your performance. But for you, it's important to feel appreciated and know that you feel acknowledged for being good at what you do. This may lead you to jobs like sales and marketing positions, which frequently reward their top professionals with awards and honors.

ASK YOURSELF
How important is recognition from my peers, company, or industry?

Travel

You may want a job that requires travel. While this may be a chance to take a trip, it's important to remember that a work trip is not a vacation. Many companies will send their employees across the globe for work-related travel that may include meetings and networking.
Business trips are solely for work or business purposes, but may lead to industry gatherings, networking events, and company events that allow for relaxation and socializing. Many industries and jobs involve occasional or frequent business travel. If travel

is something that you are not willing to do, then it's important to find out before moving forward with taking a position.

Are there any travel requirements for the position? Will I be happy traveling to work...how far and long is too much?

Contribution

Creating a happy and positive workplace remains one of the biggest challenges that companies face, but contributions made by both employees and employers can make a big difference. Some factors that can be contributed by an employee are productivity, positivity, and creativity.

What can I contribute to the company? How can this job engage my creativity?

Commute / Work from home

An important factor to considering when accepting a job offer is the commute involved. Commuting is when you travel between your place of residence and your place of work or study. When accepting a job offer it is important to determine if the commute is worth it. There are a lot of factors to take into consideration regarding commuting, including time and cost. Although public transportation is convenient, it can become costly and drain you.

Working from home, also known as telecommuting, gives employees the opportunity to work from their place of residence. When telecommuting, the employee will not have to commute or travel to their place of work. The employee "commutes" through online links and keeps in touch with their teams through telephone, online chat programs, video meetings, and email. Working from home has become a natural practice for many companies that do not need to maintain retail or public offices.

If you want to work from home full time, you can, as this was not seen as the norm before the COVID-19 pandemic, but is becoming the preferred option for many companies.

Where do I prefer to work from–home or office, or hybrid?

Lifelong learning

The learning doesn't stop when you find a job, it actually begins. There is always much to learn, and one must remember that learning is essential to succeed. Learning in the workplace improves employee performance and makes them more knowledgeable. Workplace learning can be the reason for a company's success, or can also be the reason for a company's downfall. Learning can be conducted through training courses, but employees also have the ability to learn daily through videos, or even just observing the person next to them.

Continuous learning in the workplace presents an opportunity to expand the skills and knowledge of employees. If you want to continue learning at a rapid pace, work in a company that values and provided continuous learning opportunities. You can find out about them at the company's human resources web pages, typically under the corporate heading on the website. Look for benefits such as tuition assistance and certifications.

ASK YOURSELF
Will this job and organization fill my thirst
for new knowledge and learning?

Work hours

Work hours play a major role in one's happiness because they take your time away from other things in life such as family, friend, hobbies, and relaxation. There are several types of work schedules, but the most common one in full-time office settings would be 9 a.m. - 5 p.m. That is considered a 35 hour work week with 7 hour days and one hour for lunch typically. A schedule of 9 a.m. - 6 p.m. is a 40 hour work week, both are considered "full time" hours but one schedule is a five hours longer work week.

Work hours required by a job are typically included in a job posting or announced during an interview. It's important to know the required schedules before deciding on a job. As we work from home, work hours have shifted and now the time between work and home has blurred, leaving many folks working longer hours than if they went to the office.

Keep in mind the work hours needed for a particular position and how it will affect your life at that time. Burnout is real and stress can hurt you, so keep your work hours under consideration when taking a job.

ASK YOURSELF
What are the real hours of a potential job, considering things like travel, overtime, and events?

Legacy

Almost everyone wants to leave a legacy somewhere in life, so what better place than the work environment? The legacy that is left by an employee at the workplace has to do with what was accomplished. In order to ensure that a legacy is left, figure out what you want to be remembered for and then learn the skills you need and apply them to the best of your ability. Doing your best at something that you are passionate about, and treating people well is the best way to gain legacy.

ASK YOURSELF
What do I want to leave behind after this role?

Stress

Everyone who has been employed at some point in their life has encountered work-related stress or pressure. Any job or task can become stressful, even if it's something that a person is passionate about. Common sources of work-related stress include an excessive workload, low pay, few opportunities for growth, and lack of motivation from managers, co-workers, and subject matter.

Stress in the workplace can be common, but it is important to take care of it before it progresses. It's important to establish boundaries and take time to recharge through meditation, exercise, stretching/yoga, and escaping jobs that give you too much stress.

ASK YOURSELF
What are the stresses of this job going to be?
Can I handle them and stay healthy?

Balance

A job can become very consuming, but there are ways to maintain a healthy work-life balance and find the happy medium. When you have a healthy work-life balance, you are able to prioritize your job and personal life equally. Finding balance is important in order to maintain health and sense of well-being. You will not always love a project or job, but remember that you can always escape and gain balance.

What are the responsibilities of this job going to be? Can I balance them and stay connected in my relationships and health?

Career happiness checklist

So, here's your first exercise; you'll make a career happiness checklist. Immediate happiness is easy to find. Sustaining it is more challenging. But finding happiness is a case of "to have or to have not". The career happiness checklist compiles the things that you could get out of your career life and job at one particular time in your life. Using the checklist, begin to rank the items (1's are important, 5's are less) in order of perceived happiness value.

EXERCISE (1A) - HAPPINESS CHECKLIST

Once you have completed the checklist, highlight the items that have the highest ranking (1s, 2s,). These are the things that you will try to look for at your first or next job that aligns with what will make you happy right now and into the future.

HAPPINESS CHECKLIST

Rank these career happiness elements in order of importance

(1 is most important - 5 is least important)

- Money/salary

- Work hours

- Commute time

- Fame

- Health benefits

- Tuition remission

- Training and certification opportunities

- Vacation time

- Sick Time

- Autonomy (working on your own)

- Low Stress level

- Professional Recognition

- Growth

- 401k/retirement plan/pension

- Misc

(Write in what's missing)

(Write in what's missing)

Next chapter: Compensation
Now that you understand what could make you happy in a job,
we'll explore how you get rewarded for work with compensation.

Notes

Chapter 2.
COMPENSATION
Your happiness payout.

Chapter objectives
- Understand compensation elements
- Identify benefits, perks, and salary ranges
- Calculate salary estimates

Know what you need to live happily
Most people will have different goals when it comes to desired salary, but it's important to understand the other elements that come with salary, all of which make up compensation. There is no one answer to how much money a person needs to make in order to live. Each person has different priorities that will impact this number. Some people will have financial obligations, which can include rent, automobile payments, commuting expenses and more. It is important for you to make enough compensation to live and feel good about your worth. But remember, expenses change as you get older, so the goal is to increase salary and compensation with each job.

The compensation you want and get will bring you satisfaction in a job. When your compensation needs change, it means your happiness needs are changing and it may be time for a new career experience.

Understanding salary
While researching different jobs and industries, one thing you should look at carefully are the numbers. The quickest way to do this is by searching for a specific job title or industry along with the words "salary" or "compensation" at www.bls.gov. This tool will provide a quick snippet of information. Private sector jobs consist of workers employed through individual business owners, corporations or other non-government agencies, like IBM or Amazon, for example. These jobs include employees across industries such as manufacturing, financial services, communications, hospitality, legal services, and others across every occupation.

Government jobs include a wide range of careers including working for an agency like the CIA, FBI, or Homeland Security, or working in a government office of institution such as the Post Office or court systems. Some examples of state government jobs are school counselors, police officers, firefighters, and social workers.

Hourly pay against total package

When an employee is paid hourly, they are compensated at a set hourly rate. This hourly rate is multiplied by the hours worked during a pay period. Hourly employees get paid only for the time spent working. This paycheck can sometimes be inconsistent depending on the number of hours worked weekly.

Total package, also referred to as total compensation, includes an employee's salary in addition to any benefits being received. Benefits within a total package typically include bonuses, commission, paid time off, and health insurance. Total package differentiates from a salary due to the fact that salaries include only the money that the employee is being paid.

Salary vs. hourly pay

Use BLS.gov to get salary ranges for any occupation. You can look up any occupation and view salary data, including hourly pay for freelancers or employees. The salary employee typically works without the time-clock running. Meaning if you stay late or have a deadline that causes you to work the weekend, you won't get paid any extra. If you are an hourly employee, you get paid for the hours you work, but these positions typically don't come with top level benefits, such as salary jobs. Things like medical benefits, sick leave, and vacation time come at higher volumes when someone is on salary and are included in the total package. Freelancers typically do not get health benefits through their clients so you need to secure them through your own plan or another employer.

Here's a good way to figure out salary vs. hourly wages quickly. If the job is paid by salary, take the annual salary and divide it by two. That will give you an approximate estimate of how much you get paid hourly for a 40-hour week. So, a $40k annual salary equates to around $20 per hour. If you are an hourly employee or freelancer, double the rate and get the annual salary equivalent, based on a full work week of 40 hours or so. This means that a $30 per hour freelance job estimates to a $60k per year job, considering the same amount of working hours.

FIGURE 2-1: Occupational Outlook Handbook showing job and salary data. www.bls.gov

Volunteer

A person who volunteers is undertaking a task at no cost. The work that is being completed by the volunteer is not an obligation and isn't required. The time dedicated benefits another person, group or organization. Volunteering can not only make a person feel more fulfilled, but can also look good to an employer. The more a person volunteers, the more benefits they'll experience in learning, service, and empathy.

Intern

Internships are part-time or full-time positions that are typically offered to students who are undergoing a degree. Interns apply to these positions in order to get some exposure and experience in a particular industry or field. This type of employment can be paid or unpaid, depending on the employer. An intern has the opportunity to work alongside professionals in the industry and learn from them in a working environment. Internships can play a big role when it comes to looking for a full-time job after completing college. Some can even lead to full-time positions within the same company.

Freelancer

When a person is a freelancer, they are working for themselves, rather than being employed by a company as a full-time staff member. A freelancer is self-employed and isn't committed to an employer exclusively. This type of employee has the ability to work on several projects or jobs for multiple clients at one time. Most positions that can be done as a full-time position can also be undertaken by a freelancer. Freelancing is a great way to generate extra income as well as gain experience in a specialization.

Part timer

A part-timer can be described as a person who works part-time. A part-time position requires employees to work a lower number of hours than a full-time position would, which is typically between 30-40 hours a week. Part-timers are not usually eligible for benefits, such as health insurance, paid time off (PTO), paid vacation days, and sick leave. They are paid hourly.

Consultant

Consultants are known as experts in their field. They are freelancers essentially and provide recommendations and may have skills and experience in research, project management and design in a particular area. A consultant can help someone or a company solve problems they cannot resolve on their own. While a consultant can provide advice to a person, they can also provide help to organizations in order to improve their business. Consultants typically get paid by the project or hourly.

Full timer

A full-time employee works between 30-40 hours a week. But many work even more. Full-time positions typically come with benefits that may not be offered to part-time employees. These benefits can include health insurance, paid time off (PTO), paid vacation days, and sick leave.

Tenured

When an employee is tenured, they are given a permanent

position through a contract. After working for a company for a number of years, tenured employees are valued and committed to working for the same company for a long period of time. When an employee has been with a company for more than five years, they are considered long-tenured employees. Those that have been with a company for less than five years are considered short-tenured employees.

In schools and colleges, courts and the military, tenure allows lifelong employment as long as the employee meets certain requirements and milestones to achieve tenure. Teachers and professors, and certain judges and political appointees work in tenured positions.

Benefits and perks

Employee benefits, which are compensated items given to employees, and perks (like a free tee-shirt with a company logo), are provided to workers in addition to salaries and raises. Benefits may include things such as medical and health insurance, vacation days, sick days, tuition, life insurance, and retirement benefits. Employee benefits are important not only for the employee to receive, but for the employer to offer. They provide economic security.

The most important compensation benefit next to health insurance is a retirement account. There are different retirement accounts depending upon the job you have and the organization that you work. Therefore it is important to have a basic knowledge about pensions, 401Ks, and 403Bs.

401K OR 403B

Many companies will offer employees a 401k or 403b plan, which are qualified tax advantaged retirement plans. When it comes to differences, 401(k) plans are offered by for-profit companies. For-profit companies don't have the ability to offer a 403(b). 403(b) plans are offered to employees of non-profit organizations and the government. Some of these non-profits include schools, hospitals, and religious groups.

401k – If you work for a public or private company that is for profit, then you typically are offered a 401k, which is a retirement account that you save money in and in many cases is also contributed to by the employer as a % match. So, if you contribute $100, which was 5% of your paycheck and you get a 5% match, your company would put in $100 to the account to match your investment.

403b – If you work for a non-profit organization, then you typically are offered a 403b, which is a retirement account that you save money in and in many cases is also contributed to by the employer as a % match. So, if you contribute $100, which was 5% of your paycheck and you get a 10% match, your company would put in $200 to the account to match your investment plus provide an additional equal investment.

Pension

A pension is a type of retirement plan that provides a person with monthly income once they retire from working. Money is contributed by an employer while a person is still working and is paid to them when they retire. A pension is usually distributed as a monthly check. This amount of money received is based on factors such as age, compensation and years with the company or institution. If you work in government or for the state, you may get a pension. Teachers, police officers, state and government workers get pensions. Union workers in state and private sector jobs within trades such as electrical, plumbing, and garbage disposal also can receive pensions.

Stock options

When employees have a stock option, they are presented with the opportunity to buy shares of company stock at a certain price, for a certain period of time. Stock options allow employees to feel like partners in the business. They also are a great way to secure compensation that goes beyond just a salary.

Health benefits

Although companies are not legally required to offer all employees health benefits, a majority of companies add in as part of the total package. Health benefits, or health insurance, pays for some or all of your health care costs. This includes medical, surgical, and sometimes dental expenses. These benefits are covered by the employer, but can also be deducted from the employee's paycheck. This is the most important benefit to seek as you grow older and health care becomes more critical. I always recommend to my students to only take a job in their new careers that offers health benefits.

Tuition remission

Tuition remission, also known as tuition reimbursement, is an employee benefit offered by some companies. Through this benefit, an employer pays for a predetermined amount of education credits or college coursework, which is applied towards a degree. This benefit is useful for employees looking to advance their education.

Vacation days

After working for a company for a certain length of time, employers will grant paid vacation days to their employees. Some employers will give vacation time to only full-time employees. There is no universal set amount of time that employees are expected to receive and each company is different. Paid vacation days per year increase as an employee grows and stays with the company. The typical starting vacation is two weeks per year.

Days off

Days off give employees the chance to step away from the demands of work and take some time to themselves. Through paid time off, employees can take days off if they are sick, taking a vacation, or just taking a personal day.

Free perks

Also known as fringe benefits, many companies will reward their employees with perks like free lunches, paid-for vehicles, phones, health club facilities, and more. These are great ways to keep employees happy and keep them engaged. But, this keeps you at work longer.

Home budget checklist

The best way to understand how much money you will need to make at a job is to try to determine your expected expenses as you leave college and begin your work life. To do this, you can make an expense spreadsheet to estimate what you need to live happily and pay your bills.

EXERCISE (2A) - BUDGET CHECKLIST

Using a spreadsheet application such as Microsoft Excel or Google Sheets, list all the potential expenses you may have as a working professional. Everyone's living habits are different, so the list we offer here provides some typical expenses. You need enough income to pay for these items when you are living completely on your own.

Monthly budget sheet

RENT
(a place to live that is not free - remember to
add in utilities: electric, water, cable)

$ _____

FOOD & DRINK
(eating at home, eating out, and take out, - add beverages)

$ _____

HEALTH CARE
(medical insurance and medicines/treatments)

$ _____

CHILD CARE
(taking care of children if needed)

$ _____

ENTERTAINMENT
(subscriptions, travel, weekly outings)

$ _____

TRANSPORTATION
(car payments, insurance, repairs, fuel, /mass transit, ride shares)

$ _____

COMMUNICATIONS
(smart phone, paid apps, games, streaming services, music, wifi)

$ _____

MISCELLANEOUS
(gifts, charity, unexpected expenses)
$ _____

Total estimated expenses per month

$ _____

Next chapter: Research
Now that have a sense of what might make you happy and
how you can get compensated, it's time to perform industry
and job research to discover where opportunities exist
and what evidence you need to project to get them.

Notes

Chapter 3.

RESEARCH
Finding viable job opportunities.

Chapter objectives
- Understand the job hunt game
- Identify company websites vs job boards
- Apply job research techniques
- Analyze job descriptions, keywords and phrases
- Create new opportunities through continued skill building

Playing the job game
Searching for a new job can be both exciting and frustrating at the same time, but hard work pays off in the long run. I have been teaching career skills to people for a long time. Even when I wasn't a teacher, I helped friends, family, coworkers, and clients with writing cover letters and resumes. The first thing that I always did when I began to teach students how to create their resume is to get them to focus and have confidence.

Creating a resume and portfolio should be an opportunity to reflect on your abilities. You get to know yourself, and what makes you relevant professionally. Everyone has some experience and skill that makes them valuable. The trick is recognizing or acquiring those abilities and then matching them to a career. If you are confident, you will be able to focus better on the tasks at hand. Confidence comes with eliminating the unknowns. If we know our skills and abilities and we know what makes us happy, we can then match that to a career path. The career path you pick should be based on happiness. That's why in many instances throughout your life, your path changes. That path can include entrepreneurship, corporate, freelance, or philanthropic pursuits. It doesn't matter what you want to do in your career. The important part is taking the steps needed to promote yourself so that you can get there. Your resume, cover letter, and portfolio are career communication documents to help in that journey, and research is vital to making them effective.

Self esteem and self actualization
Although they sound similar, self-esteem and self-actualization are two different concepts, but both can directly impact the

other. According to Abraham Maslow's hierarchy of needs, these two concepts are what motivate people at the highest levels. Self-esteem refers to the overall feeling of self-worth. It's important to have high self-esteem, especially when looking for jobs. This will lead to self actualization.

People that are self-actualized feel more fulfilled than those who are not. Self-actualization is the drive pushing a person to fulfill their full potential.

How does this all relate to you, the job seeker? Self-esteem gives a sense of who you are and that your skills matter in the world, regardless of what they include, how good you think they are, and how you can use your skills to help others. Self-actualization is who you become by using those skills, in your own eyes and to the professional world. For example, if you want to be a filmmaker, and have created some short films at school or on your own, introduce yourself not simply as a student or new graduate who makes films (self-esteem), but as your professional role in society, as a filmmaker, (self-actualization).

Company websites

When it comes to applying, are job boards like Indeed and LinkedIn the most effective way to apply to a job? If you guessed no, then you're correct. Many companies will post job openings on multiple platforms in order to reach a larger audience, or even a specific kind of audience, but the most important asset to utilize would be the company site. Company websites will store your information, which gives you the opportunity to receive a call back for other opportunities, if they arise. When applying on a company website, you are competing against a smaller pool of applicants, which naturally decreases competition. There are a lot more people applying through job boards than directly through the company website itself.

It's also important to deliver your credentials to employers in their preferred format. External job sites may utilize other formats, which may not be preferred by the company itself. Some companies also provide more detailed job descriptions on their websites, compared to the descriptions posted on job listing sites, or by recruiters.

If you are looking to stand out amongst other applicants, apply on company websites to ensure that your credentials are being sent directly. Job boards or recruiting agencies often have a middle man, which can complicate the process. There are several ways to go about finding company websites. If you have a particular company in mind, the simplest way to research is to do a Google search of the company along with keywords, such as "jobs." Searching and learning about companies can also show these recruiters that you have an interest in their company. Recruiters are far more likely to pursue a candidate that is knowledgeable about the company or industry, rather than someone who shows little interest and may not be applying for the correct reasons.

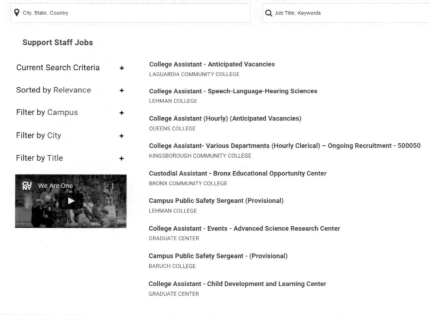

FIGURE 3-1: CUNY company website job postings page. www.cuny.jobs. The CUNY.edu website has jobs for all the (CUNY) City of New York University, across all occupations and all campus locations. There is a university system in each state, which allows you to apply to jobs at all campuses in the system.

Industry job boards

If you have started your job search, then you are most likely familiar with job boards. A job board is a website that is used by employers to promote job openings to those that are seeking employment. Job seekers can use job boards to search for opportunities in their industry and profession. Job boards are valuable tools for recruiters and hiring managers. In just a few clicks, these sites give employers access to an abundance of potential candidates. An industry job board example is aicpa. org, which is the website for the American Institute of CPA's. This site offers a job board for accountants. Virtually every industry has trade associations that provide specialized job boards.

Niche job boards

Niche job boards are typically smaller websites that are focused on a specific industry or location. These job boards help target those candidates that are more qualified and fit the specific role. Niche job boards make it easier for candidates to discover new companies, as well as new job openings. Niche job boards range from sales, to education, to media and so much more. For example, if you search "account coordinator" on any job board, you'll come across hundreds, if not thousands, of results in every field. Niche job boards allow job seekers to find exactly what they're looking for in terms of positions, and also allows companies to target the exact candidates that they need in order to fill these roles.

FIGURE 3-2: Niche job board for media and communications jobs. www.mediabistro.com

LinkedIn job listings

LinkedIn is a powerful tool when searching for a job and building your career. It is the largest professional network on the Internet and acts as a social networking site for the business community. LinkedIn can be used for a variety of things, such as finding the right job, connecting with professionals in a variety of industries, and learning skills that one will need to succeed in their career. Users can create a professional profile that acts as a resume and reference sheet all in one.

Members can view your profile and learn more about an individual's business background, areas of expertise, and groups or organizations that they belong to. When using LinkedIn to look for jobs, a person can include in their profile whether or not they are seeking new opportunities. LinkedIn's job feature allows users to search through a variety of open positions posted by a company. Users have the opportunity to apply and fill out applications either on the job posting directly, or will be redirected to the company's website. The application and the applicant's LinkedIn profile are then sent directly to the potential employer.

Bridge, foot in the door, and dream jobs

While researching and looking at specific jobs, three types of job opportunities are the bridge job, foot in the door job, and dream job. It's important to distinguish between them. Each one may lead you to different career opportunities.

A "bridge" job can be referred to as one that you may take while transitioning to a new job. Bridge jobs get you from one place to another. They are typically building blocks towards your next job. These bridge jobs can be part time or internship gigs that give you some money and experience. Foot in the door jobs are opportunities that may not rate as high on the happiness checklist as you would like, but they help get you in to an industry or company that you plan to move forward with in the future. Both bridge and foot in the door jobs can help you learn the industry, build your skills, make connections and discover your next opportunity. For example, if you're looking to make the switch from sales to hospitality, you may look for an entry level position in sales, such as a Sales assistant, that may not be your dream position, but will help you land that dream sales manager position in the future.

We all have different ideas and definitions of what our "dream job" may be. A dream job sounds exactly like it would be. It is the one that connects you with your self-actualization. This is the job that you dream of in a perfect world. It's important to wake up in the morning and enjoy what you're doing. For some people, a dream job might mean a nice paycheck, a big title, or a specific work culture, but to others it could be a fulfilling role that helps people, regardless of status or money.

People have different priorities and expectations when it comes to what they want out of their jobs, but it all comes down to one thing. When working in your dream job, you are loving what you do and supporting the lifestyle that you choose to live. You will know when a job is right for you.

Not sure what job is right for you? That's where research comes into play. You have the ability to expand your knowledge through research. By doing so, you can find out what you want in a job and what you don't want, the industries you are interested in, and the stuff that excites you.

Industry research

As complicated and tedious as it sounds, we perform research daily whether we know it or not. This type of research is referred to as everyday research, which sounds pretty straight forward. When we are looking up where we should grab dinner from, we are performing everyday research. The same efforts should be put forth when looking for a job.

When performing research, questions come to mind about the unknown and bring a level of clarity to our ideas. Research is a tool that can help us get ahead and can be an advantage when applying for jobs or seeking career opportunities. This is an essential step in the resume and cover letter process. Research provides you with the information you need to target your resume and cover letter to a specific industry. It will also help you build your portfolio and help you figure out what should be included and what can be left out. Researching industries, jobs, and skills will help you make sense of your career search options at the moment.

Government and industry data

As you begin your career search, you'll learn about the kinds of jobs that are available, or learn about different industries that may spark your interest. Industries are broad and contain many sets and subsets of career opportunities and jobs.

When searching for that "dream job," it is important that you look into the industries that really excite you. Each industry consists of factors and features that will either appeal to you, or may not be your type, but that's why it's important to do your research. It's important to be interested in what you are doing. A great place to find industry information is at company, industry, and government websites. The Bureau of Labor Statistics Website located at www. bls.gov provides overviews of careers across industries and provides some great baseline information on skills, salaries, employment forecasts, and specific job descriptions within the industry.

Industry association sites provide background information of the industry with career resources and job listings (Public relations - PRSA.org, Broadcasting - NAB. org and Advertising - AEF.org are examples).

Industry research will lead you to job research. This is where you build your knowledge about what jobs are available in certain industries and determine the skills and experience needed to gain a certain job and build or continue your career.

Not sure what industry is right for you? Get started at: http://www.bls.gov/bls/industry.htm

Check out the U.S. department of Labor's Career Guide to Industries at www.bls.gov/oco/cg/home.htm. It provides a list of major industries that you can then view individually to find demand, salary, and skills data.

Also of great value is the Occupational Outlook Handbook at https://www.bls.gov/ooh/
Find the fastest growing and highest paying jobs data here.

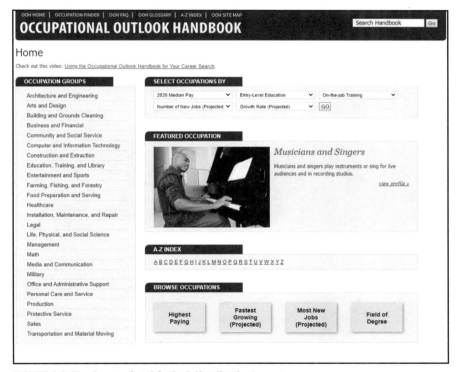

FIGURE 3-3: The Occupational Outlook Handbook at www. bls.gov offers key data on salaries and trends

Job posting analysis

Job research is a process of finding and analyzing job postings. Every job posting will require skills from the candidate, and you must remember that skills make our applications stand out from the others. Employers separate potential candidates by evaluating skill levels in addition to experience. Even though a candidate may not have experience in a particular job, they may have skills to do that job, which could allow them the opportunity to land the role and build experience.

The skills needed for a job are often listed prominently in a job ad. To understand the terminology in the ads, refer to industry websites, books, or talking to industry people in order to figure out what skills are needed for a particular job. You can begin to narrow down your research to see exactly what your options are once you inventory your own skills.

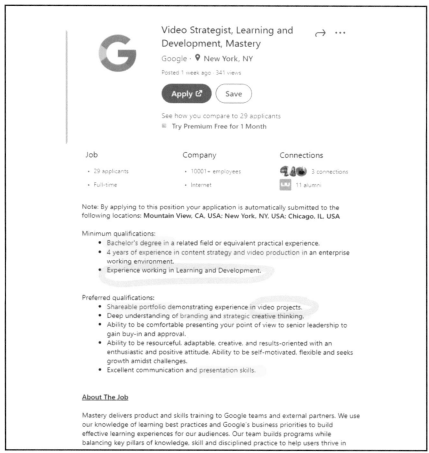

FIGURE 3-4: Analyzed job description focusing on keywords and phrases.

Identifying keywords and phrases

When applying for a job online, many applicants tend to just quickly submit their resumes and cover letters and then move forward. That is a huge mistake. When applying Online, there is a high chance (95%) that your application will go through a software applicant tracking system first, before being reviewed by a human recruiter. These tracking systems screen and sort through resumes by keywords and key phrases. In order to make sure that your application stands out and makes it through the screening process, you should tailor your resume to match the keywords in your resume to the job description that is provided by the employer.

It all starts with the job description. It's important to understand what the employer is looking for in a candidate and what the position requires. The first thing that should be done when coming across a job posting that you want to apply to should be highlighting key words. Jot down a list of major keywords that come across as being important.

After highlighting and getting a sense of what the position calls for, you should go through your resume and ask yourself, "Do I have the experience that this employer is looking for?". With the description available, it is important to show the employers that you are a match. After going through your resume, the next step is updating it and adding in keywords in important sections, which include your profile, skills and experience.

Once your resume is gone through and tailored to fit a job description, it is important to proof and save your updated resume and repeat the same steps when it comes to another job description.

Recruiters and hiring managers have a tendency to quickly go through your resume, so it's important to make sure that you have what will focus on their needs. Tailoring your resume to match the job description plays an important role in securing a call back.

EXERCISE (3A) - JOB AND KEYWORD LIST.
Find real jobs descriptions and fill in the industry, job
name, and keywords and phrases you find.

Start: Go to the website www.BLS.gov.
Steps:
1. Using the search box, research industries and list job names
and associated keywords. Create a list of industries, jobs, and
keywords that interest you. The keywords are especially important
because you will use them in your resume and cover letter.

Look for job descriptions directly...Look at 2-3
industries, and find job descriptions

2. Use the chart below to build a short blueprint of which
industries contain attractive jobs and freelance opportunities.
This will allow you to narrow down specific positions to focus on
during your job research. Enter important keywords for skills and
experience. You will be matching these to your personal abilities
later on in the planning process. An example is provided.

Industry name	Job name	Keywords

Industry name	Job name	Keywords
Media and Entertainment	Copywriter/Editor	Work on small and medium-sized multiplatform campaigns and single ads; event and marketing collateral; name and tagline generation; scripting (live and video), mid- and long-form editorial pieces and more. Collaborate to conceive and develop original, creative concepts rooted in strategic foundation
Media Streaming	Paid Media Associate	Support all media trafficking needs by scheduling and maintaining placements, rotation of ads, and creative throughout the lifetime of campaigns Develop and test new audience segments (i.e. retargeting, lookalikes, custom audiences, etc.)
Agency	Art Director	Drive high level concepting, tactical program ideation and polished design for a wide range of marketing outputs from short-form video and interactive web experiences to social content and experiential activations

Finding keyword matches

Once you're done researching the industry, the next step is job research and actually look up job descriptions on company, industry, and LinkedIn job sites that have the keywords and phrases you need for your resume. You won't apply just yet, but will learn about what they are seeking to find a match.

Most company websites will have a "careers" tab, usually at the bottom menu. Here is where you can find jobs that may interest you, then answer the questions below to help yourself "make sense" of the potential job or career opportunity. Job and skills research allow you to look at the jobs within industries so that you can discover if they are a match for you and potentially something that you want to pursue. It's important to look for matches in ESP – Experience, Skills, and Passion.

There may be some skill gaps when comparing the description to your job experience, but not every requirement has to be met. Put yourself out there, but be realistic in your pursuits. Skills can outweigh experience in the knowledge economy, so always be on the lookout for keywords that may fit your experience.

Experience:
- Is the job suitable for my current experience level? If not, what experience is needed?
- Is this a "foot in the door" opportunity where experience is not as critical as skills?

Skills:
- Do I have the listed skills needed for this job? Which do I have and which are missing? Can my skills make up for a lack of experience?
- Will I be able to learn new skills at this job? What are they?

Passion:
- Is the job aligned with my happiness list? What are the positives and negatives?

- Is this a "bridge job", "foot in the door", or a "dream job"

EXERCISE (3B) - SKILLS AND HAPPINESS WORKSHEET.

Next complete the worksheet below to help visualize and quantify the jobs you found during the research phase. Particularly, what skills do you need? And, what are the potential positive and negative happiness items connected to each job and industry? This worksheet will help you to see what aspects will be positive and which will be negative. Ultimately, no situation is absolutely perfect so the goal is to have more pluses than minuses.

JOB RESEARCH: SKILLS AND HAPPINESS WORKSHEET

Job Title Company Industry	Job/Opportunity Type D (dream) B (bridge) F (foot in the door)	Skills required (use keywords)
My Skills	Happiness Grade (+) (highest ranking items) (Pro's)	Happiness Grade (-) (lowest ranking items) (Con's)

Copyright © 2013. DiMarco Associates, LLC.

SAMPLE

JOB RESEARCH: SKILLS AND HAPPINESS WORKSHEET

Job Title Company Industry	Job/Opportunity Type D (dream) B (bridge) F (foot in the door)	Skills required (use keywords)
Senior Manager of Marketing Tarte Cosmetics Cosmetics	D	-Exceptional analytical and creative skills - Excellent written and verbal communication skills - Strong interpersonal skills and ability to work collaboratively across all departments
My Skills	Happiness Grade (+) (highest ranking items) (Pro's)	Happiness Grade (-) (lowest ranking items) (Con's)
- Good problem solver - Great interpersonal skills and able to work collaboratively - Creative - Am able to work independently	- Dream industry - Pays well - Medical insurance - 401k - Commuter Benefits - Mid-Senior level job, room to move up if I wanted too	- Easy commute (in NYC) - I wanted to get out of NYC

Big four hard skills

Having the "Big Four" hard skills in your tool belt can be valuable as you apply to different jobs. These skills are things that you can do to produce something tangible. They include research, writing, speaking and design.

Research SKILLS

Research skills are vital in information jobs. Employers want you have the ability to find answers to questions. Research refers to the ability to search for information and use this information to gain knowledge. When a candidate is capable of performing research, they are able to better understand and apply in-depth information to solve a problem. This skill set enables people to identify a problem, collect information that can help address the problem, evaluate resources and analyze proposed solutions based on data. Research using Web data tools like Google analytics is critical to creating and launching websites. Research on partner companies, competitors, and products is used by businesses in every industry.

When talking and writing about research skills, be specific and discuss the research goal, how you collected data, and which tools you used for analysis and presentation.

Writing Skills

Writing skills play a critical role in communication across our public and private lives, and during interactions with coworkers, clients, partners, and other stakeholders in our lives. Strong writing skills are often linked to thinking skills. It shows an attention to detail. Whether you're applying for a job, writing for a blog or social post, authoring a book or article, or simply writing a business letter, the ability to communicate clearly with words on a page is one of the most valuable skills you can have. One good way to be a better writer is to read extensively. Read a wide variety of both fiction and non-fiction items, especially the type of works that you would like to write in your career.

When talking and writing about writing skills, be specific and discuss the process you went through (interviews, observations, commentary on experience) what types of pieces you wrote, who the audience was, and where the work was published (if so).

Speaking Skills

As a professional, it is important to be an effective speaker and presenter so that you can convey information to small teams and large groups. Public speaking skills and the ability to present information publicly are in demand across a wide range of industries, especially those that are searching for leadership positions and client contact roles. In your career, there will be situations in which you need to speak in front of a group, whether it's your coworkers, clients, or a group of strangers. It is important to keep in mind the delivery, but also the takeaway – so practice your speaking and presenting skills through platforms including social media and through person video analysis, where you record and watch yourself "perform".

Design/technology skills
Design skills are used to solve problems. Technology is used in the design process at some point to produce both preliminary and final solutions. For example...A resume, an advertisement, a marketing campaign, and a website are all products of human design using technology tools. The ability to design things is critical in a content and problem driven world.

We are all designers, constantly solving problems with creative projects. Design is about making things that have meaning as a solution. If you have completed a project or made something, you have designed. With design skills come the ability to use tools and technologies. Auto mechanics use sophisticated computer software to diagnose vehicle problems.

Graphic artists use programs like Adobe Photoshop to create artwork used in packaging, products, publications and anything printed or on-screen. Accountants and managers use applications such as Microsoft Word, PowerPoint, and Excel to create business documents. YouTube creators and advertising teams create clips and shorts using video editing software and digital cameras.

When talking and writing about design skills, be specific and discuss the problems you engaged, how you designed the solution, and what the design deliverables were at the end of the project.

Soft skills in communication
Soft skills are always in-demand and are important qualities in job applicants. Soft skills are communication skills, – they describe how you work and interact with the people around you effectively. Your communication skills, your work ethic, how you treat people, and professional attributes (eagerness to learn, passion for the

field) will ensure growth in the workplace. Soft skills in and out of the workplace are more critical than ever before. These set of skills equip you with ways to remain efficient and productive.

Intangible skills

Of course, there are always the "intangible skills", which should be part of your overall skill set and be included in your interview discussion. These skills include being team oriented, a problem solver, a multi-tasker, dedicated, and detail oriented. These items are "a given" in today's workforce. The skills are not always taught, but often learned and obtained from personal experience.

The best communicators have a skill that puts them above the others. They listen. The easiest way to build trust with an employer, or coworker, is to show interest . This can be done by simply listening to what others have to say. A good listener doesn't have to think about what they are going to say next when the other person is speaking. When in doubt, turn to cues like "tell me more." It's important to show someone that they have your full attention and every word is being taken into consideration.

Time management is essential when it comes to being efficient. When someone has good time management skills, this person knows how to manage their time in a way that is more productive, more efficient, and is more likely to meet deadlines in a timely manner. Time management in the workplace maintains productivity and keeps a boss happy at the same time.

It's important to be creative in the workplace, which can include finding ways to solve problems with limited resources or making things. Creative thinkers have the ability to design and develop something new. Employers in all industries look for new ideas and perspectives into the workplace. A creative workplace inspires a team to work with each other. When applying for jobs, highlight your ability to not only think as a creative person, but to also use your creativity to solve important problems using design and technology tools.

Being organized in the workplace can increase productivity. When someone is organized, less time is spent looking for things and more time is dedicated to getting a task done. Organization skills help keep you focused on different tasks, and use your time and energy effectively and efficiently. It can improve the flow of communication and work between you and your team, which makes work less stressful.

Identifying skill gaps

"Skill gaps" is the phrase that is commonly used to describe the difference between the skills that employers are seeking in an applicant and those the candidates looking for a job actually has. When going through applications, an employer may not hire a specific candidate due to skill gaps. Employers identify skill gaps in order to ensure that their workforce is knowledgeable, well trained, and the most equipped to perform the job.

You may find yourself looking for career opportunities in areas that require you to gain new skills, which may require some learning. As someone who is just diving into the new full-time routine, there may be skills asked of us by a particular job ad description that we may not have, but that doesn't mean that we can't obtain them. Along with skills that we don't currently have, there may be some that we aspire to have. We have the ability to learn on the job and pick up or polish the skills that we need.

To identify your skill gaps, you can go to information sources including government and industry job information websites (like www.bls.gov). Look at the pages that describe "typical skills" to see if your skills match what is called for in these industries. Another place you can find the required skills for a job or particular industry is by looking at job ads at company websites.

The "job ads" usually provide a bullet list of skills and experience that is expected for candidates applying for a position. Also, talking to people in the industry can help reveal soft and intangible skill sets needed that are often known in that particular industry or job. Things like having a "thick skin", or the ability to "deal with the politics" in the workplace. It is important to connect and network with others in your industry and ask questions. This can be done by email or through social media sites, such as LinkedIn, Twitter, or Facebook. By doing so, you can receive advice that will help you recognize critical hard and soft skills for an industry.

Building skills

Building skills is not something that happens overnight. It's important to implement the skills that we learn in order to become more comfortable with them. Practice makes perfect. Your personal tool belt is what will stand out to employers and put you ahead of other applicants going for the same position.

When building skills, it is important to make sure that you have the "big four" under your belt, which include: speaking, writing, design/technology, and research. These four skills are essential and can help you move into a wide variety of careers. They are valued in every job and industry, especially professional positions.

COLLEGE COURSES
You can take college courses and secure a degree. This is one of the most effective ways of building skills and it often provides high grade opportunities for learning such as internships, practicum, and skill-based courses. A college degree has much value in the information-based jobs economy that we live in. Many Fortune 500 companies won't hire professional employees without a college degree. If you have a degree already and need to polish your skill set, you can also take college courses as an audit student, which means that you attend on a non-matriculated (no degree sequence) basis. This allows you to take the courses that you need and shorten the time span in college.

CONTINUING EDUCATION AND TRAINING COURSES
Many colleges have continuing studies programs that provide short courses in industry specific areas. These courses provide ample information and many are skill based so that you can get a good orientation to a skill and then you can practice to further build it. Training courses also provide concentrated skills in virtually any area that interests you. You can attend training centers that are privately operated and there are also training programs at many libraries, high schools and colleges. Check the Websites of the local schools, colleges, and libraries in your area to see what programs exist.

TRADE SCHOOL
This is a great choice if you want to work in the professional service industries that deal with construction, repair, manufacturing, and building. These schools can provide skill-driven educations, provide required certifications, and offer transitions to apprenticeships and job opportunities. This type of education is a good stepping stone to owning your own business in a trade.

SELF-TEACHING - BOOKS & ONLINE

You are always learning, but can intensify the experience by exploring learning on your own. You can get books and online instruction from Google, Microsoft, and Adobe, as most software makers offer a full suite of tutorials. You can also look at online YouTube videos, as well as find e-learning courses from a wide range of college and high school providers. Many low-cost online educational opportunities available also offer certificates and industry credentials so that you can have your professional level training verified by companies, again check out Adobe, Microsoft, and Google first.

FINDING MENTORS

Mentors are all around you. They are the people who teach you things in everyday activities. You can pick up life and career tips if you listen closely to others, especially those whom you respect and admire. Look to family members, internship supervisors, professors and teachers, coaches, co-workers, friends and bosses. These are the people in your life that will teach things without you even realizing it.

INTERNING, VOLUNTEERING, AND APPRENTICESHIPS

Interning and volunteering allow you to perform industry, job, and skills research all at once. Internships provide the opportunity to work and learn, minus the paycheck usually – although paid internships do exist.

Many companies will hire interns from colleges, but some companies will also consider hiring interns as trainees. These foot in the door jobs are highly valuable when you are skill building. Apprenticeships are usually available in trade areas and typically do carry some wages. They offer you the chance to explore the on-the-job day to day work routine while you learn the trade skill. Apprenticeships often lead to union memberships, which provide a level of security for future career opportunities.

PRACTICE

Once you learn new skills, you need to practice them regularly; otherwise, you will lose them over time. This is true with technical skills, such as using software and physical skills like welding. Practice is inherently important because industries and skills change. We need to change and adapt our skills as time and technology progresses, otherwise we become obsolete. Technology forces learning and makes us servants of practice, if we want to stay relevant. Skills can be self-taught. I first learned how to use computers and design software by making menus for my brother-in-law's pizza place.

So volunteer to make stuff for people and learn while you are doing it. Explore the specific tools you need and want to use in your career and life. Books, e-learning courses, tech equipment, teaching materials, and other resources are all readily available on the Internet. Make self-directed learning a lifelong process.

Developing your brand plan

Finally, the culmination of your research and self-evaluation should be organized into a brand plan that you can use when you interview and network. You may be new to your field professionally, but you need to "act as if", which means you are already aligned with your career, regardless of the stage. The brand plan helps you isolate your value and also allows you to communicate that you are constantly learning to understand the technologies and skills that you need to be even more valuable to your clients, employers, and industry.

EXERCISE (3C) - BRAND PLAN

Now, you will create a brand plan that provides a clear outline for you to use when you are networking, interviewing, and self actualizing. It allows you to isolate your skills and identifies how you can help potential employers. The approach acknowledges your skill gaps, explains how you plan to address them with continued learning, and provides an opening to ask to continue the relationship.

Act as if…define who you are	Where can you help?	How can you help?
I M A _____ specializing in _____, _____, and _____.	**MY BENEFITS** I can help people and organizations in the areas of: _____ _____ _____	**MY SKILLS** My skills include: _____ _____ _____ _____
Where are you growing?	How are you going?	How do you promote your personal brand? Which of these promotional documents are you using?
MY FUTURE I am building my skills in: _____ _____ _____ _____	**MY PLAN** To build my skills I am: _____ _____ _____	**MY INFORMATION** Thank you for your interest in me. Please let me give you my [ ] Resume [ ] Cover/pitch letter [ ] Print portfolio [ ] Web portfolio URL [ ] Business card [ ] Social media site [ ] Event date [ ] Published Articles [ ] Blog URL [ ] Video URL

Sample

Act as if…define who you are	Where can you help?	How can you help?
I M A graphic designer, specializing in manipulating images using Adobe Photoshop, creating professional layouts using Adobe InDesign, and developing creative solutions for clients.	**MY BENEFITS** I can help people and organizations in the areas of: -small and medium sized campaigns -creating creative strategies for media -researching target audiences and new target markets	**MY SKILLS** My skills include: -Problem solver -Organized - Ability to work with others and independently -Time management -Ability to stay current with technologies, social media, and trends
Where are you growing?	How are you going?	How do you promote your personal brand? Which of these promotional documents are you using?
MY FUTURE I am building my skills in: -marketing -advertising -design principles and concepts	**MY PLAN** To build my skills I am: -researching social media trends -learning how to reach certain target audiences -working in a team environment	**MY INFORMATION** Thank you for your interest in me. Please let me give you my [X] Resume [X] Cover/pitch letter [X] Print portfolio [X] Web portfolio URL [X] Business card [ ] Social media site [ ] Event date [ ] Published Articles [ ] Blog URL [ ] Video URL

Next chapter: Resume

You have begun to establish the criteria for finding happiness at a job based on a range of different happiness elements coupled with compensation to help prove your worth. Next you will learn about how to make a powerful resume that will elevate you toward an interview and eventually a job that want or need.

Notes

Chapter 4.

RESUME
Design and write with intelligence.

Chapter objectives
- Understand resume types, content, and design
- Connect your job research with your resume
- Identify KSA's (knowledge, skills, and abilities)
- Define resume headings for maximum matching
- Write engaging action and success content
- Write and design an intelligence resume
- Create a reference sheet

The intelligence resume defined

The intelligence resume is one that's based on pinpointing organizational and job requirement similarities and exploiting them in your resume. Creating an intelligence resume means that you are using content and design rooted in science, research, technology, and industry best practices. I call it the intelligence resume for two reasons, first, because creating it requires using "intelligence" (or intel), which is data that leads to decisions, gathered through research on the industry, the occupation, the organization, and one's own reflection of professional value. Second, because it highlights you from the crowd through content and design, it allows your "intelligence" to be completely promoted.

A critical review of empirical research by the author on resume content over the past 35 years from computer science, information science, applied psychology, business, communications, career science, personnel psychology, and social psychology were used in determining how to create the intelligence resume format. As well, the most recent industry-based data from studies published in business and news periodicals was reviewed and incorporated. The intent is to leverage science and research to help gain an edge in creating an effective resume.

KSA'S – knowledge, skills, abilities

Ultimately, the resume allows the candidate to make a connection, and then further bolsters their case for employment in concert with industry-based conversation in an interview and project-based evidence in the form of a portfolio, work samples, or possibly a skills test. That's why the intelligence resume focuses on presenting content that has been shown in research to influence managers, including the fit between KSA (knowledge, skills, and abilities) and job requirements. KSA's are described inthe job description. Knowledge resonates from experiences, skills pertain to your application of a technique or tool, and abilities are the core competencies you have to use those skills and that knowledge in a job. KSA's are transferable to multiple occupations – always remember that when changing positions or careers. You don't start over, you just grow your KSA's over the course of your life.

Attraction-selection-attrition model

Researchers in applied psychology have found that work experience and educational background are positive influences on the perceptions of hiring managers and recruiters when judging the abilities of job applicants, which means that KSA's should be heavily present in resume content. As well, the intelligence resume takes into account the attraction-selection-attrition (ASA) model, which argues that organizations seek and select candidates who portray similar attributes found in particular candidate job experiences, extra-curricular activity, volunteer work, and industry affiliations.

The key to the intelligence resume is the research behind your resume content and making it "fit" the recruiter and organizations similarities.

The intelligence resume is not based on anecdotal advice or assumptions from the past. It discards the boilerplate approaches that put form over function, which in their own vanity and lack of audience catering fail to match what is needed in the information economy. You must have keyword driven skills, results, and experiences, which are the ingredients to the mission of solving problems and completing projects. Resumes need to be based on science, not just stories. The resume is mission critical to getting the job that you want in an industry that will engage your mind and body toward a happy state.

It's important to remember that creating a resume requires understanding your industry, the organizational audience and the technologies that are used to select candidates for an interview. The clear focus on simplicity, connectedness, and similarity-rich verbs in the intelligence resume accentuates accomplishment, ability, and viability, highlighting your strengths as the right person for the job and attracting the organization to see how you fit their needs and mission.

Resume value

The resume is the most important business document in your life and it will be an important part of self-promotion throughout your career. The resume promotes you, your skills, and experience and should be directed at a particular occupation, project, or business opportunity. Resumes can be used for more than just job hunting. They offer a clear document that acts like a fact sheet, listing only the relevant information that has value to the receiver. So, this means that your resume can be used for self-promotion in a wide variety of venues including internships, awards, college applications, volunteer work, consulting opportunities, and also for securing freelance work. Resumes are typically one to two pages. For new graduates and students one page is recommended.

Matching keyword criteria

The words you use in your resume content matter. The content of the resume, in the form of keywords and key phrases, is recognizable and searchable SEO - search engine optimization. SEO provides a tool for data collectors to filter out the most relevant words that match the job prospect to the job description. Their presence becomes critical in getting someone, or software, to match you with a potential job. Looking at the way applicants are sorted and dismissed due to a lack of KSA's gives us insight into how we should use keywords in resumes. Let's trace back how a job becomes a posted job that someone can apply for after reading a job description.

Here's the typical sequence of events that leads to the job posting you would see on job boards like Monster or Indeed, or on a company website. A "hiring manager", in some capacity, that could be as high as the CEO, will have a need for a person to fill a role. Assuming a new hire is approved by the manager or board above, the manager will typically submit the job description to the human resources department to create a new "line". A "line" is short for the term budget line item. This means that the company has money in their budget to pay for a new employee. Once approved, a line becomes a job posting. Job postings are created based upon what the manager and the organization need in a new hire. The first place the job description gets posted is the company website and then to any other digital channels for collecting resumes from potential candidates.

Job descriptions carry keywords and phrases that can be used in writing resume sentences by utilizing parallel construction. Parallel construction of sentences is a technique for including the subject criteria, in this case the job description, into the final text to run "parallel" to the requested items in the job description. Then, by using action verbs, persuasive, value driven sentences can be constructed.

Applicant tracking systems

Although they all end up in the same basket eventually, the freshest jobs are on the company website, not Monster, Indeed, or LinkedIn. Regardless of where you submit, your information is filtered and stored electronically. Once you submit your resume, especially in mid to large organizations, the resume goes through an Applicant Tracking System (ATS). Taleo, from Oracle is one of the most widely used. These software systems collect and funnel resumes into a massive database. They also process job applications from large pools, and allow candidate searches based on keyword matches to assist human resource departments and their respective hiring managers in the hiring process. It has been shown that 95% of mid to large companies use applicant tracking software to filter resumes.

The system collects your resume from somewhere that you applied and send it to a digital collection box where it is ranked based on criteria from the job description against the other candidates. ATS systems also help with the recruiting process and hiring functions. Because job postings are now online rather than in newspapers as they once were, they are much longer and more semantically descriptive, which points to the need for intelligence resumes.

Mission critical keywords

Keywords, considered content in resumes, are the KSA

(knowledge, skills, and abilities) based words in a job description. The text in the job descriptions, the "keywords" are matched to the text in the resume that you submit. Therefore, you need to be careful when performing what is known as "keyword packing", which are techniques for extracting the vital words from the job descriptions and pack them into the resume text. Research supports direct keyword usage in resumes, but industry articles and eye tracking studies recommend keyword packing with care and craft using parallel construction that utilizes action verbs in context. This is because someone, rather than software, will be reviewing your resume eventually as you move through the process. We don't want to be copying directly from job ads as it will hurt our professional appeal.

This is a writing challenge as we need to inject keywords and phrases coupled with success verbs as best as possible, while maintaining clear, understandable language in the active voice. Do not blatantly plagiarize the job advertisement. Instead, the parallel construction of keyword-rich phrases sets off language matching, which triggers response mechanisms from ATS software and steely eyed managers as they are both seeking the specific KSA's that meet the criteria.

Finding the right words and translating them into the resume initially requires sound research to uncover the keywords, phrases, and parallel language that have true value and will resonate with the various receivers. Applicant Tracking Systems are binary machines, either the exact word or phrase is present or it is not, so you will need to have isolated the correct phrases and proper spellings for the keywords, as terms must be exact to the character, otherwise they can be missed by the software bot. – Remember to refer to the job descriptions of jobs that you want to figure this out, which offer the keyword data, as we learned in the previous chapter on research. If you have not completed the previous chapter, please stop here and review it before starting to create your resume. You need to perform research to get the data to create an intelligence resume – otherwise, you'll just be guessing!

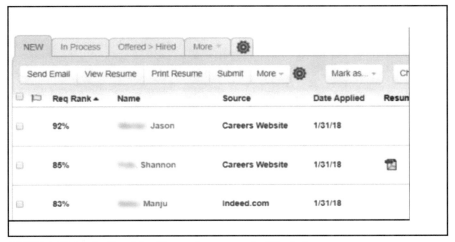

FIGURE 4-1 Taleo Applicant tracking system screenshot illustrates the candidate ranking, which is based on job description criteria.

F-pattern and eye tracking

The science behind how a recruiter reviews a resume, what they look at, where they look on the resume, and how much time they may spend reviewing the document is measured in eye tracking and web usability studies. Eye tracking uses heat maps to locate where readers are reading on a screen. Usability tests how usable a device or document is in delivering communication and allowing user actions. Researcher Jacob Nielsen and other researchers including Shrestha, and fellow researchers studied usability in document and web design and described the "F" pattern reading style as standing for "fast", as in fast visual consumption of text in the content area on the left side of the page. The value of the F-pattern design is consistent with how folks read and scan a document on the screen.

In a 2006 study and then a 2020 update, Nielsen used eye tracking to determine how a reader reads a page. Nielson's theories on F-pattern reading have been tested and confirmed by other researchers. He found that by using heat map tests on where the users' eyes go, he could determine where information is absorbed the fastest and most frequently when reviewing a text-based web page. The results from 2006 stayed consistent in 2020, with the

F-pattern as a typical response to engaging with web content.

The F-pattern works with the content on the page as the magnet for the eye. Nielsen and others confirmed that horizontal movement occurs first across the top of the page section, which is the first element in the document or the top of the "F" line. Then the reader moves down the page to the set to a shorter area than the previous reading, which is the lower line in the "F". The reader concludes the view by scanning the left side of the document vertically, typically in a slow systematic way or a faster review of the left side heading, which are the stem in the letter "F". The main idea here is that vital information needs to be in the "F-zone", which is the top and second line of the invisible "F" pattern that is used in a layout because users can't stop themselves from reading this way according to researchers. The F-pattern causes some implications for the reader which Nielsen, et al. (2020) describe as "the first lines of text on a page receive more gazes than subsequent lines of text on the same page". And "the first few words on the left of each line of text receive more fixations than subsequent words on the same line". These scientific observations are helpful in how we layout the resume to meet the viewers' tendencies.

Another source of eye tracking information is offered by a job board and recruiting organization called The Ladders. They execute and the Internet publishes eye-tracking studies based on recruiter actions and preferences. They do this to present data on trends in resume consumption and to better inform clients and candidates on how to create their resumes according to the data they gather. In the Ladders 2018 eye tracking study, their data showed that recruiters in 2018 spent 7.4 seconds on average screening a resume, their data previous to 2018 stated that recruiters spend 6 seconds or less on reviewing a candidate's resume. Their study also offers some guidance on good resume design and creating a layout using an F-pattern. As noted above, resembling the letter F, the F-pattern is a layout that weighs the most important keywords at the top of the resume and uses clearly marked sections and title headers to lend seamless structure to the document. Researchers advice on the value of the F-pattern also recommend that you provide an overview or mission at the top of the first page, which is what we have described in this text as an objective, profile, or profile with appended objective. This data further reinforces the need for the important part of the F-pattern of text.

By following the resume writing and design instructions in this book, you will be creating your resume using the F-pattern layout. As well, the template included uses the F-pattern to help you get started quickly by simply filling in your information to a pre-formatted document with defined style sheets and visual structure.

Resume design

Business communication research tells us that companies use software to store, analyze, and recommend candidates based on keyword matches. However, we still must design our resume so that it works on a piece of paper first, as well as the screen. This guides content suggestions for resumes. What about layout and visual design? Does it really matter if I use a cool font that I like, rather than a standard font? Or, can I create a cool design for my resume, with two columns and plenty or lines to break up the section, maybe make it in color? Research informs us that these are bad ideas. We know that resumes are electronically collected, stored, and analyzed before human eyes glance at them, so the goal is making them beautifully simple for consumption for both people and machines. This requires the resume to be appealing both software algorithms and scanning human eyes.

I have formally studied graphic design, written about it, taught it, and performed it for the past twenty plus years. Throughout, the idea of "simple" has always challenged and inspired me to focus on refinement and reduction, attempting in many projects to marry minimalist sensibilities with maximum communication value. This is also the goal for resume design. I declare to my students who come to me with over designed resumes that – simple is the new fancy, and we must strive for it. Then, I guide them on how resume design affects the perception of machines and people.

Reducing the clutter will help the communication greatly, but you must practice design restraint, first by not using the provided templates in Microsoft Word as the communication design within them opposes good design practices and research driven formatting on resume, which we offer below. We provide a resume template for you that is designed and driven by science and industry on the book website, so you have design assistance if you need it.

THE CASE AGAINST "FANCY RESUMES"
Now, being a creative myself, meaning that I work in production

and design, making and creating content, I realize that some positions may ask for a "design resume", also known as the "fancy version". And that is okay, but you should have two resumes in that case. The intelligence resume is a design resume. I support this because it shows consistent typography and the beauty of simplicity in visual communication. But if you must create a fancy resume, with non-standard fonts, multiple column layout, and color, make sure to be wary of the value of good communication and the power of simplicity. This book offers one approach to resume design, based on published research and industry studies. I don't suggest using a "fancy resume", either, but if you are asked for a "design resume", there are many recommendations and samples on the web for making one.

BEST PRACTICES FOR RESUME DESIGN
Study after study recommends against designing the resume with paragraph-based text, as we now know through eye tracking and keyword analysis, machines and people prefer simplicity in information gathering. With bullets as a design feature in your resume, you achieve ordered taxonomy of KSA's (knowledge, skills, and abilities) for the reader, so always use bullets over bulky paragraphs. As far as ornamental stuff like rules, underlining, vertical separator lines, and thick section underlines, they hurt the design and hinder absorption of data according to the research.

Recommendations from research point to these considerations in resume design to help achieve precise recognition from both software scans and hiring managers:
- Place your name at the top of the page on its own line. (Your name can also be the first text on pages two and three.)

- Use standard address format below your name, list each phone number on its own line

- List your email address and social handles on separate lines

- Use an F-pattern layout with profile and skills in the "F-zone" of content consumption
- Employ white space and consistent margins

- Black and white only - no color or photos (unless a talent job)

- Use standard headings and subheads

- Use bullets, not paragraphs

- All text left justified, even the name section.

- Use familiar, clear typefaces such as Arial,
  Times, Helvetica, and Times New Roman

- Use a font size of 9 to 13 points for bulleted blocks and
  headings. Use style sheets to maximize consistency

- Don't use condensed or extended spacing between letters

- No photos, logos, or icons

- Use font size and boldface to highlight section
  headings. Think hierarchy of text for sections.

- Avoid all fancy type treatments such as italics, underline,
  shadows, and reverse (white letters on black background)

- Avoid vertical and horizontal lines,
  graphics, and boxes around text

- Avoid two-column format , don't create a
  resume that resembles a newsletter

- Be ready to submit the resume as both a Microsoft Word and
  document (.DOC) or in Portable Document Format (.PDF)

Remember you should not use the blank resume templates offered
in MS Word or any other program. This book has a downloads
section and website that provides clean templates. The templates
allow you to create a beautifully simple resume, using "intelligence
resume design" on your own, which will empower you for the rest
of your professional life. People and software engines reviewing
resumes and hiring you do not give style points. Companies
routinely ask candidates to copy and paste their resumes into a
form so that all the formatting and clutter can be stripped away.

Hiring managers must make decisions on content
about skills and experience, so we must get those

pieces to them as quickly and easily as possible. Proper typography and text layout are critical to doing this. Most books on resumes give you literally hundreds of resume examples, which overload your brain and confuse the design process with personal style. You need only one design style, the intelligence resume design.

EIGHT REASONS TO USE THE INTELLIGENCE RESUME DESIGN:

1. Uses the F-pattern layout preferred in eye-tracking tests

2. Uses one font with varied styles to create a simple, consistent hierarchical design

3. Uses Arial or Times New Roman fonts to allow uniform appearance across computers and formats

4. Easy to copy and paste into submission fields without font or alignment problems

5. Maximizes the 7-8 viewing seconds the average recruiter skims your resume

6. Creates structured hierarchy of text providing easy visual digestion

7. Easy to update consistently when jobs and computers change

8. Appropriate for most industries and positions

Mary Smith

2 Half Hollow Place
Niagara, NY 00000
671-000-0000
msmith@mail.com
linkedin.com/marilynsmith
marilynsmith.mywebsite.com

(A)

Profile

Event management specialist with experience developing large scale projects for corporate and non-profit events. Seeking to utilize my skills and experience in public relations, advertising, and marketing to benefit a flourishing organization.

Skills

(B)

- Ability researching venues and scouting locations for large and small events.
- Experience producing promotional flyers and social content using Adobe Photoshop.
- Proficient developing client pitches and presentations using Microsoft PowerPoint and Word.
- Fluent using research tools including databases, search engines, and indexes.
- Strength writing corporate communications materials including fact sheets and business letters.

Experience (C)

Assistant Events Coordinator   January 2018 – Present
Berry Black Event Company, Madison, NY
- Responsible for building client databases via phone and email.
- Assist in booking private parties and events for over 100 guests.
- Serve over 50 clients per event in a fast-paced setting.
- Develop seating charts and agendas for 5 events per week.

Account Coordinator
FreshClick, Inc., Madison, NY   October 2016 – December 2017
- Personal assistant to two agency owners working with high profile clients.
- Supported tabletop sessions at product launches, fundraisers, and trade fairs.
- Performed administrative duties including bookkeeping and managing phone calls.

Cheerleading Coach
Manor Public Schools, Manor Cove, NY   January 2017 – August 2017
- Trained and coached athletes in cheerleading ranging from ages 12 – 18.
- Managed the financial budget saving 10% on expenses over one year.
- Organized local competitions and exceeded fundraising goals of $1000 per event.

Education (D)

Bachelor of Science in Mass Communications (B.S.)   May 2016
Niagara University, NY
- Dean's List   (E)
- Varsity Cheerleading Team Scholarship

Associate in Science in Liberal Arts (A.S.)   May 2012
Niagara County Community College, NY

FIGURE 4-2: Intelligence resume design anatomy. (A) big pockets of white space. (B) common heading names including skills (first), experience, education (last) (C) Hierarchal type with position first, then company (D) education listing degree and letters (B.S.) (E) Dates to the side and smaller to downplay inexperience.

Resume chronology and functionality

Resumes can be formatted any number of ways. Functional resumes are heavy in listing achievements, skills, and coursework. Chronological resumes are focused on listing work experience in a time-based order. The research says don't commit to either fully. Use a combination of both for maximum impact and communication. It is important that you provide skills and achievements, as well as job listings and accomplishments, complemented by education using a reverse chronological order, which is the most recent information that comes first. This approach can be tailored to your background and experience. If you have not had much work experience, you can complete the resume with items such as relevant coursework, volunteer work, memberships, and special projects.

Resume length

In my experience and according to the research, resumes should be two pages maximum. One page is appropriate for new graduates and students seeking internships. So, your first resume should be one page.

Most job seekers should use one page and more experienced (5 years+) professionals may have two pages. In many cases, the resume needs formatting and revision to get it to the proper length. Why only one or two pages? This is because hiring managers need to grasp information about a person quickly and fluidly. What you don't want is a page and a half – either one full page, or two full pages.

I have heard cases where people have not been allowed to submit a resume over a page. If you feel that you need a lengthier resume because you want to include many sections and deep chronology, then you should consider creating a curriculum vitae (CV) instead of a resume. Some recent studies have touted longer resumes beyond two pages, but this comes with a gamble as clarity and simplicity will always be in fashion in career communication. But as noted previously, always make sure a CV is preferred by the hiring manager before sending, which would typically be requested in the job description.

Resume preparation

The process of creating a resume is about gathering information and presenting it in an orderly, understandable way that offers facts. All your experiences, across your professional life count. They inform the recruiter about specific experiences. But they also create unconscious perceptions on similarities and attractions between you, the organization, and the recruiter with regards to interests, perceived values, and integrity. These shine through with the types of positions held, the organizations you helped, and in other experiences like volunteer work. When similarities exist, persuasion is heightened, so be sure to inventory all that you have done since high school and work back in reverse chronological order, with the most recent experiences first. If older experiences don't fit into the one- or two-page format, that is okay as you will be editing down the text to remove the clutter and outdated material.

To prepare to create the resume, previously in this text, you performed job and industry research, which will help you establish KSA's that the organization and industry are seeking in qualified candidates. You'll transfer the information from the previous job research exercises when you write your resume bullets. But first, you need to collect the basic demographic information about your experiences and education, which require you to have accurate dates, locations, and titles of positions and degrees earned.

Information collection

Jobs, internships, and volunteer work are all considered experience, which will yield Knowledge, show application of Skills, and promise of critical Abilities (KSA's).

Don't worry about the bullets yet, we'll do that later in the chapter, but for now get the critical base information.

Jobs:
Information about all jobs you've had, including company names, contact names, job titles, and dates of employment. These can also include other positions held in performing independent projects and events.

Internships:
Information about internships (unpaid) you've had, including company names, contact names,

department titles, and dates of employment.

Volunteer:
Information about volunteer positions you've had, including organization names, contact names, positions, and dates of employment. List the locations of any volunteer venues and briefly note what you did to refresh your memory for later (served food to seniors, for example)

Education:
Relates to learning experiences and accomplishments that you have earned through a third party (school, association, government, media). Information about any schools you've attended, including school names, locations, graduation dates, specific degrees earned and GPA.

Also include here any teams you were part of or Greek life involvement. Include study abroad trips here and any certifications you received from an industry or academic institution. Be sure to add in any certifications or training badges you received for learning online through a company (Google Analytics course, or CPR certification, for example)

Finally, make a list of relevant courses that directly connect to the job you are seeking. For example, if you are going into public relations or communications, you would want to list skills courses such as public relations writing and communication strategies.

Remember - only list your last college. Meaning if you are in high school, don't list junior high school. If you are on college, don't list high school. But you should list both undergraduate and graduate college degrees. If you went to one school for a few semesters and transferred to a new college, list the most current school, not the one you left.

Awards:
List any awards you may have received or activities you may have been involved in with dates. This could be scholarships, work citations, or special recognition for an event or participation in something within an industry.

Resume typography

This section shows you how to make your resume in a step by step format. We explain each piece of the resume so that you understand why and how to create each part.

To create the resume, we will start with each section, format the fonts, save the style to the style sheet and then move to the next section.

You can type your information right over the text in our template provided in the downloads section to maintain the style and layout.

Once you have one section complete, you can copy and paste it to create a new section by updating the text, which will keep the formatting. Or, you could type the text, highlight the lines and apply the styles from the styles palette in Microsoft Word. Either way, you will format and save the style for further use in the document, which allows maximum consistency.

We will present each section of the resume systematically, together in the chapter to build the intelligence resume with an eye to both content and design.

FONTS

Pick one font family, either Arial (or Helvetica) or Time New Roman (or Times) for the entire resume. A font family consists of the various styles of that font, which may include bold or italic. Use these fonts in different sizes and styles. For emphasis, use bold. For secondary information, you can use italics (not to much!) or even better, just use a smaller font size to create hierarchy. But, never use underline because it makes type look gross by cutting off the descending parts of the letters.

Use the same font sizes for each section. Consistency is critical to making the resume read well and look good. Try these initial font and style suggestions:

ARIAL:

24 point bold main section heads

12 point bold main section heads

10-11 point subhead (could be **bold** or *italic*)

9-10 point body copy (never **bold** or *italic*)

8 point dates (**bold for long sentences**)

TIMES NEW ROMAN:

24 point bold main section heads

12 point bold main section heads

10-11 point subhead (could be **bold** or *italic*)

9-10 point body copy (never bold or italic)

8 point dates (**bold for long sentences**)

No color on fonts, black text on white works best. Another formatting rule is single line spacing throughout and only a single space after a period.

BULLETS
Use bullets consistently and appropriately. Avoid the automatic bullet feature in MS Word or Google Docs. It creates poor spacing and wastes valuable F-zone real

estate on the page. Instead, create your own bullets.

Three ways to make bullets on a computer:
1. MAC Desktop or Laptop: Option key + 8
2. Windows Desktop: Hold ALT and the press 0149
on the numeric keypad on the keyboard.
3. Windows laptop (no numeric keypad) uses the character
map in the accessories folder. Choose bullet (alt+0149)

Resume page formatting
The page should be set up with margins at .5 or .25 (1/2 inch
to 1/4) all around. Next, you'll create each section and then
record the style in the style sheet so that you can use the
same font consistently without worrying about formatting.

Use style sheets for fast updates
Style sheets are a great tool for consistency and easy updating.
Create styles and apply them in the resume. Use a basic hierarchy
to set up the first sections and then simply apply as needed.

Don't worry the formatted templates provided with
your book purchase have style sheets embedded.
Instructions on how to download them are at the
end of the book in the Resources section.

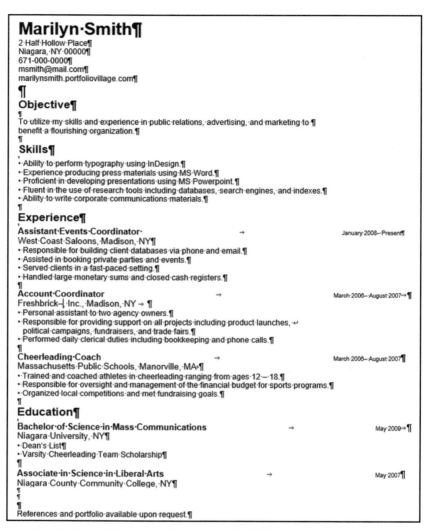

Marilyn·Smith¶

2·Half·Hollow·Place¶
Niagara,·NY·00000¶
671-000-0000¶
msmith@mail.com¶
marilynsmith.portfoliovillage.com¶
¶
Objective¶
¶
To·utilize·my·skills·and·experience·in·public·relations,·advertising,·and·marketing·to·¶
benefit·a·flourishing·organization.¶
¶
Skills¶

·•·Ability·to·perform·typography·using·InDesign.¶
·•·Experience·producing·press·materials·using·MS·Word.¶
·•·Proficient·in·developing·presentations·using·MS·Powerpoint.¶
·•·Fluent·in·the·use·of·research·tools·including·databases,·search·engines,·and·indexes.¶
·•·Ability·to·write·corporate·communications·materials.¶
¶
Experience¶

Assistant·Events·Coordinator· → January·2008—Present¶
West·Coast·Saloons,·Madison,·NY¶
·•·Responsible·for·building·client·databases·via·phone·and·email.¶
·•·Assisted·in·booking·private·parties·and·events.¶
·•·Served·clients·in·a·fast-paced·setting.¶
·•·Handled·large·monetary·sums·and·closed·cash·registers.¶
¶
Account·Coordinator → March·2006—August·2007→·¶
Freshbrick–|·Inc.,·Madison,·NY·→·¶
·•·Personal·assistant·to·two·agency·owners.¶
·•·Responsible·for·providing·support·on·all·projects·including·product·launches,·↵
   political·campaigns,·fundraisers,·and·trade·fairs.¶
·•·Performed·daily·clerical·duties·including·bookkeeping·and·phone·calls.¶
¶
Cheerleading·Coach → March·2006—August·2007¶
Massachusetts·Public·Schools,·Manorville,·MA↵¶
·•·Trained·and·coached·athletes·in·cheerleading·ranging·from·ages·12—·18.¶
·•·Responsible·for·oversight·and·management·of·the·financial·budget·for·sports·programs.¶
·•·Organized·local·competitions·and·met·fundraising·goals.¶
¶
Education¶

Bachelor·of·Science·in·Mass·Communications → May·2009→·¶
Niagara·University,·NY¶
·•·Dean's·List¶
·•·Varsity·Cheerleading·Team·Scholarship¶
¶
Associate·in·Science·in·Liberal·Arts → May·2007¶
Niagara·County·Community·College,·NY¶
¶
¶
References·and·portfolio·available·upon·request.¶

FIGURE 4-3: Microsoft Word formatted resume with hidden characters showing the consistent styles.

Resume writing

Now that you have learned the focus of the intelligence resume in content and design, I will walk you through the process of creating your intelligence resume. Each step builds a new section of the resume. It considers both writing and design in the process, as both are equally important in gaining a successful match on a submission.

STEP ONE - YOUR NAME HEADING

This heading should be exactly the same on the resume, the cover letter and the reference sheet. For an online resume connected to a Web portfolio, don't include home address and telephone number.

Here's what goes in your resume heading, each on its own line:
Your name
Address
Tel
Email
Portfolio URL (if you have one)

Social handles (LinkedIn, YouTube, Instagram) – use your professional social media accounts only, unless you are going for a job in social media, then you may need to provide all your handles.

Mary Smith

2 Half Hollow Place
Niagara, NY 00000
671-000-0000
msmith@mail.com
linkedin.com/marilynsmith
marilynsmith.mywebsite.com

FIGURE 4-4: The resume name heading.

STEP TWO - THE OBJECTIVE OR PROFILE

Several articles I recently reviewed on professional resume writing do not recommend placing an objective on the resume. Authors claim that using an objective is outdated. The peer reviewed research I uncovered showed that profiles or professional summaries are preferred for high level candidates over objectives. However, research also shows that first time candidates or new graduates can still use an objective, with recommendations to focus on injecting keywords and offering value to the organization, rather than hoping to get something from the experience.

One more nuanced solution is to use a combination of both, which is... use a profile that appends an objective as a last sentence – what I call the appended profile. Ultimately, you will decide which one to use on your resume based on your experience level. The standard recommendations I on objectives and profiles...

- internship applications use objectives only
or profiles with appended objectives
- new graduates and experienced professionals can have profiles or appended profiles, but not objectives only.

Let's go through the objective, the profile, and the appended profile to understand each and how to construct them.

OBJECTIVE

Resume objectives need to directly point to how you can help the organization. I see many students with a resume objective that is selfish. The reality is that no one is going to hire you based on the fact that you want to "learn and grow". Hiring managers realize that you are applying to get a position, so don't use the resume objective to tell them again...stay away from sentences such as "My objective is to get the position of sales manager". Remember, the objective or profile will be the first data hit in the F-pattern and should be meaningful in a very compact statement.

Another way to translate these findings and advice into a good strategy is to use a profile that has an objective added at the end of the profile, which I call the appended profile. You will use the one that feels best, but I advise using the appended profile for new candidates or a detailed profile (no objective) for experienced candidates.

Objective template:
Objective: To utilize my skills and experience in (list
1, 2, or 3 keywords) _____, _____, and_____
to benefit a flourishing organization.

Objective example:
To utilize my skills and experience in marketing, advertising,
and public relations to benefit a flourishing organization.

This approach gets to the point and holds keyword value while
saying that you want to contribute. For an internship, this objective
works. It is a no-nonsense, unselfish objective that says… "I
want to help the organization with my abilities". It's a great way
to start the resume and it sets the tone for you to begin to cater
the resume to the job and the organization. You can also call it a
"career goal" if you buy into the case against the word objective
currently circulating the press. I still believe that the word objective
works for intern applications and less experienced new graduates.

PROFILE
After the first job, the objective immediately changes on the
resume to a profile. A profile or also can be titled summary, is
a brief overview of one's skills, experience, and capabilities. It
is suited for experienced people because it requires substance
and typically is centered on a particular industry or position
and accomplished in the field. Often, the profile has keywords
embedded in it so that it becomes industry specific.

You should avoid long profiles because they take away from
the other content and become a distraction. Keep the profile
to two to three sentences and write it after you complete
the resume so that you can have a sense of what you are
summarizing. Be sure to include a few keywords, the role you
want, and some achievement that presents you as a value to
the organization. If you can cite tangible, measurable items
like sales revenue, social audience increases, industry awards,
or benefited groups, the profile becomes more powerful.

Before writing, review the job descriptions and your own
personal brand plan to lend focus. The profile should be
directed toward the job you want, rather than the job you
just had, so act as if, and offer value in a way that hints
at how your experience has and will benefit others.

Profile Template:

Profile: Title you want (Marketing Director)
Dedicated and accomplished professional in the field of
_____. Successful in _____ and _____ for the
past ____ years as a _____ and _____. Provide
_____ to _____, which have yielded
_____for clients. (or - the company).

Profile Example:

Profile: Marketing Director
Dedicated and accomplished professional in the field of marketing.
Successful digital media and communications specialist
working for the past five years in social media management.

Remember, the objective or profile can be removed completely,
but research shows that either can provide a source of keyword
matching in applicant tracking systems. If you have the space,
you should include an objective if you are a new graduate
and add a profile after your first professional experience.

Finally, you can combine both, in what I call the appended
profile, to create a profile that has an objective statement
appended (on the end), which you would simply label
as profile or statement as usual. In this case, you mix
both statements, with the focus on what you can do for
the organization, with keywords as staple elements.

Appended Profile:
Title you want (Director of Sales)
Dedicated and accomplished professional in the field of
_____. Successful in _____ and _____ for
the past ____ years working in _____ . Seeking to
utilize my skills and experience in _____, _____,
and _____to help a flourishing organization.

Profile with appended objective example filled in:
Profile: Marketing Director
Dedicated and accomplished professional in the field of marketing.
Successful digital media and communications specialist for the
past five years working in social media management. Seeking
to utilize my skills and experience in marketing management
and e-commerce to help a flourishing organization.

Marilyn Smith
2 Half Hollow Place
Niagara, NY 00000
671-000-0000
msmith@mail.com
marilynsmith.portfoliovillage.com

Profile
Dedicated and accomplished professional in the field of marketing. Successful digital media and
communications specialist for the past five years working in social media management. Seeking to utilize my
skills and experience in marketing management and e-commerce to help a flourishing organization.

FIGURE 4-5: The resume profile

STEP THREE - ADD SECTION HEADINGS

You should determine your resume section headings carefully. You should not list many sections with little substance. Use a good balance of 3-4 bullet points to round out each section. So, for resume sections such as work experience, where you list jobs and projects, you should have two or more bullet points and no more than six or seven. If you don't have at least two sentences, then that information should be deleted or connected to another section. If you have more than six, you are not being concise enough and need to edit down to use parallel construction to textually match job requirements.

Below, you'll find a list of sections that can be used in your resume. You may have another section idea in mind, that's okay as long as it can be filled with at least two bullet points and of course it should be relevant to the job or career opportunity that you are pursuing.

List the sections in an ordered outline form and then under each enter the demographic information, which includes the information gathered at the preparation phase including school name, graduation dates, job title, company names, employment dates, and locations. No need to write the descriptive sentences yet, you will do that in the next step. For now, begin to decide on sections and list the basic information. You can always add, delete, or combine sections if needed so pick sections that you can fill initially.

The suggested resume sections are in this order:
Objective or profile (taught & completed above)
Skills
Experience
Education

Main section headings

Below, we detail the main section headings with a summary of what should be included. You can use the standard four above or add in other sections to fill gaps or describe unique experiences. Additional heading such as Relevant Coursework or Volunteer Work are okay to add if they fit. Remember to have your Objective or profile (see above for the samples) also.

SKILLS

This section is required on all resumes. Include the big four skills in some form to portray a balanced, useful skill set - research, speaking, writing, and technology/design plus specialized skills for your industry. This section is also where you would put language skills (translation or interpretation). Remember, you want the skills you list to align with the job opportunity requirements and beyond. This is vital to new graduates who don't have much experience yet, but may have a demonstrable set of skills that make their case stronger in the eyes of the hiring manager.

Always use bulleted sentences that specifically describe your skills and are "keyword-rich". These will ping the ATS system and get the reader's attention as these sit in the F-zone.

In the skills section, write out the hard skills that you have in clear terms using action-based verbs. Qualify how you can use the skill in a task. Too many times I see students creating their skills section simply by putting down names of software rather than what they can do with the software. If you can use Photoshop to manipulate and correct graphic images then you need to write that on your resume. --Always put skills in context, rather than just naming a piece of software. You would not use only the word "Photoshop" or "Adobe" in the skills section, but the context that you use Photoshop in, such as: "Experience retouching photos for social media content using Adobe Photoshop".

Same rule applies with Microsoft Office, which is really a suite of applications including Word, Excel, PowerPoint, OneDrive, Outlook, and Access. If you use certain programs for certain things, then state that fact by using parallel construction as much as possible. For example, you should write "Adept at creating and editing newsletters and reports using Microsoft Word", rather than simply writing "M.S. Office" as a skill line in the resume, especially when the job description mentions being responsible for newsletter and report creation.

Below, I offer skills descriptions that are "keyword-rich" and in the form of action verbs. You need to craft the words around the skills to give them parallel construction and relevance to the particular job. Don't over stuff keywords; use them in the context of what you have done.

Bullet examples across a variety of skills
Notice how the sentences use action verbs
with context wrapped around.

- Ability to manipulate images and color correct photographs
  and artwork using Adobe Photoshop for advertising design.

- Adept in corporate accounting and bookkeeping
  for non-profit organizations.

- Experienced in document editing and page
  layout using Microsoft Word.

- Skilled in creating business presentations
  using Microsoft PowerPoint.

- Fluent in interpretation and translation of Spanish.

- Strength in project management with multiple
  team members in the healthcare industry.

- Public relations writing skills developing press
  releases, backgrounders, and fact sheets.

- Advertising account management skills including prospecting
  and creative concept generation across financial sectors.

- Experience counseling and managing youth
  groups in educational settings.

- Analytical skills executing qualitative and quantitative
  marketing research for Fortune 500 companies.

- Management skills in budget supervision and
  purchasing for insurance and securities clients.

- Performed patient lab analysis in clinical
  settings and private practice offices.

- Experience managing construction and capital
  improvement projects for large municipal organizations

It's important that you don't pad the skills section with skills that you don't have. This can get you into trouble. Some organizations require applicants to take skills tests to prove that they have the abilities. And, a hiring manager will look at the resume if you proceed in the process so you want the writing to be original, but "keyword rich". You need to include all of the relevant hard skills that you have in the section. Hard skills are specific. For example, computer software skills include coding, web development, and mobile app creation. Marketing skills include SEO, digital marketing, product development, and e-commerce. Writing skills include persuasive writing, promotional writing, technical writing and news writing. Design skills include graphic design, UI/ UX, photography, and video creation. Management skills can include staff and project management across any number of disciplines. Other skills that have value in an information driven job market are data analysis, research skills, and social content creation – all should be relevant to the job descriptions. Look for the keywords in the job ads and then list those skills your have in your resume.

For soft skills and qualities like team work, communication, work ethic, dedication, and problem solving, you should integrate those features into the experiences section. Embed them in the bullets within the experience section sentences. You should not list soft skills in the skills section because they are typically expected. The company expects you to be a good communicator, dedicated professional and hard worker. They don't expect you to be able to code or know how to use social media platforms for business content.

Marilyn Smith

2 Half Hollow Place
Niagara, NY 00000
671-000-0000
msmith@mail.com
marilynsmith.portfoliovillage.com

Profile

Dedicated and accomplished professional in the field of marketing. Successful digital media and communications specialist for the past five years working in social media management. Seeking to utilize my skills and experience in marketing management and e-commerce to help a flourishing organization.

Skills

- Ability to perform typography using InDesign.
- Experience producing press materials using MS Word.
- Proficient in developing presentations using MS Powerpoint.
- Fluent in the use of research tools including databases, search engines, and indexes.
- Ability to write corporate communications materials.

FIGURE 4-6: The resume skills section

EXPERIENCE (WORK HISTORY AND INTERNSHIPS)
This section is required. In the experience section, which can also be called work experience, you present the most relevant experience connected with the job description. You want to reference anything that you've done previously if it relates to the next opportunity.

Many times students or new job seekers question if they should put certain jobs in this section if they don't have a connection to what they want to do. In this section you can list any type of experience. There is no need for additional headings, besides "Experience" unless the lack of content dictates those headings being needed.

In many cases, your past, parallel experience will be beneficial and should be listed. Sometimes you need to leave off certain jobs and experiences if they are too old or don't offer value to the next job, but if you don't have much content, you need to use the experience section to clarify important qualities.

Qualities such as responsibility, teamwork, dedication, and customer relationship interactions are particularly important and can be shown in the tasks you completed previously.

USING ACTION AND SUCCESS VERBS
Action verbs are the norm for skills bullets, as they offer a broad description – like "responsible for" or "experienced in". For experiences, success verbs have found a valuable place in the resume rhetoric alongside or in place of action verbs. Success verbs denote exactly that, success in some measurable way. They point to accomplishments beyond simply completing tasks. Words such as grew, minimized, built, optimized, gained, developed, eliminated, created, expanded, or established – these provide specific results. This will resonate in your application with hiring managers who are tuned in to evidence and data in decision making. You will get attention by writing sentences that illustrate success.

Success verb sentence examples:

- **Counseled** 10 youth groups through new health certifications.

- **Performed** 100 studies and reported qualitative and quantitative marketing research for Fortune 500 companies.

- **Saved** 5k in error claims performing budget supervision and purchasing for insurance and securities clients.

- **Completed** over 20 construction and capital improvement projects for large municipal organizations.

- **Grew** social media followers by 20% over a 30-day period using Facebook.

- **Earned** certification for 30 hours of industry training on safety and compliance procedures.

- **Developed** e commerce website and five user apps for a brand marketing company.

FIGURE 4-7: The resume experience section.

EDUCATION

This section is required. The education section should have a chronological listing of degrees with years and schools. For the date section on the resume, you need only put the graduation month and year, without showing the year range. If you are in college, you don't need to list your high school. Don't include your high school attendance on your resume unless you are high school.

If you have gone to college but have not earned a degree make sure that you do not list a degree, instead list as "studies". Even if you were only 3 credits short or didn't actually get your physical degree because of a hold or overdue library fees or housing fees, be truthful on all applications. It's important to be honest and accurate because it is inherently wrong to and relatively common to be revealed. If you get caught, you will be fired and your professional reputation risks being damaged, not to mention the wasted time that you put in to get the job with resume sending and interviews.

Make sure to list what degree you are getting and your concentration (if you have one), major course of study, and minor course of study. Those should be listed because a particular degree type may be required and that would certainly be in the keyword database. It also offers insight into your specializations in one or more areas, which also supports your listing of KSA's in a domain. Another helpful suggestion is to write out the degree name correctly using both the full title and the acronym for maximum exposure to ATS's (for example use both Bachelor of Science and B.S. in the text).

Education

Bachelor of Science in Mass Communications   May 2009
Niagara University, NY
• Dean's List
• Varsity Cheerleading Team Scholarship

Associate in Science in Liberal Arts   May 2007
Niagara County Community College, NY

FIGURE 4-8: The resume education section.

Here's how you would write this out in your education section:
Bachelor of Science in Mass Communications (B.S.) May 2020
St. John's University, New York, NY

Master of Arts in Communication Design (M.A.)   May 2020
Long Island University, Brookville, NY

Other items to list in education could include GPA or honors, which should be below the degree, school, and major. These can be bulleted under the degree text like this:

Bachelor of Science in Mass Communications (B.S.)   May 2020
St. John's University, New York, NY
• GPA: 4.0

- Dean's List 2019, 2020
- Recipient: 2018 Rose Marie Scholarship
  for Academic Achievement

Final preferred resume headings

The final heading design for the resume should be clear and use recognizable headings that will directly connect with applicant tracking software systems and rank your resume higher.

Marilyn Smith

2 Half Hollow Place
Niagara, NY 00000
671-000-0000
msmith@mail.com
marilynsmith.portfoliovillage.com

Profile

Dedicated and accomplished professional in the field of marketing. Successful digital media and communications specialist for the past five years working in social media management. Seeking to utilize my skills and experience in marketing management and e-commerce to help a flourishing organization.

Skills

- Ability to perform typography using InDesign.
- Experience producing press materials using MS Word.
- Proficient in developing presentations using MS Powerpoint.
- Fluent in the use of research tools including databases, search engines, and indexes.
- Ability to write corporate communications materials.

Experience

Assistant Events Coordinator   January 2008– Present
West Coast Saloons, Madison, NY
- Responsible for building client databases via phone and email.
- Assisted in booking private parties and events.
- Served clients in a fast-paced setting.
- Handled large monetary sums and closed cash registers.

Account Coordinator   March 2006– August 2007
Freshbrick–, Inc., Madison, NY
- Personal assistant to two agency owners.
- Responsible for providing support on all projects including product launches, political campaigns, fundraisers, and trade fairs.
- Performed daily clerical duties including bookkeeping and phone calls.

Cheerleading Coach   March 2006– August 2007
Massachusetts Public Schools, Manorville, MA
- Trained and coached athletes in cheerleading ranging from ages 12 – 18.
- Responsible for oversight and management of the financial budget for sports programs.
- Organized local competitions and met fundraising goals.

Education

Bachelor of Science in Mass Communications   May 2009
Niagara University, NY
- Dean's List
- Varsity Cheerleading Team Scholarship

Associate in Science in Liberal Arts   May 2007
Niagara County Community College, NY

References and portfolio available upon request.

FIGURE 4-9: The final resume sections. You can add either an objective or profile depending on your experience level.

Additional resume headings

The following headings can be used in addition to the standard headings (profile, skills, experience, and education) if there is a lack of information to fill the other sections adequately with at least 3 bullets.

VOLUNTEER WORK

This section is optional. You may want to have a separate section for volunteer work if it is something that you have engaged in at various levels. If you don't have a separate section, but want to include a few instances of volunteer work, you can place them under education. If you have a large block of volunteer work, you can include it as an experience and place it in the Experience section as if it was another job.

Volunteering for your church or school, your fraternity, or a local organization shows that you not only are anxious to use your skills and abilities but also adds value to you as a compassionate human being. Showing volunteer work on your resume and in your portfolios can be very helpful when applying for jobs in nonprofit organizations as well as larger companies that have a reputation for volunteering in various community settings.

You can list specific parallel construction of the bullets if they are in a standalone section like experience or volunteer work. Be sure to follow the bullet writing tips in this chapter.

If you have single volunteer bullets under the education section, you can list them like this:
• Volunteer: NY Cancer Society March for a Cure   May 2020

PROFESSIONAL MEMBERSHIPS

Listing professional memberships is important if you work in an industry that has intimate ties to the career opportunity you are seeking. This is especially true in areas such as education, academia, science, government, and trades. Many organizations have free memberships, or discounts for students and new professionals, which can help you get started in your industry groups. As well, join industry groups on LinkedIn to show your place as a professional in the field. These online groups can be added to the resume in lieu of brick and mortar organizations at first. If you have single professional membership's bullets under the education section, you can list them like this:

• Member: Public Relations Society of America (PRSA)   May 2020

CERTIFICATIONS AND TRAINING
This section is optional, but contributes to your KSA value.
Some career opportunities require you to have certain
certifications or training. It's critical that if you are required
to have these, you list them separately under this heading.
Teachers, medical staff, attorneys, trade people, and other
technical specialists all should list some items that show ongoing
learning in the form of continuing courses or online training.

If you have single certification or training bullets under
the education section, you can list them like this:
• Document Imaging Architect Certification (CDIA)   May 2020
• Document Imaging Architect course   May 2020

Other sub heads to weave in
These subheadings may be added if they can be justified as
relevant. Try to weave the information into another section
heading. For example, academic honors can go in the
education section. And, languages can be added to skills.
But for some items, like interests, they are not recommended
throughout the research literature and should not be used
to take up space where KSA content can be placed.

- Academic honors (add this to education if possible)

- Relevant coursework (add this as bullets under education or
as its own section if needed to fill a gap – still place it under
the Education section). You should list only core courses here
that pertain to the job or industry. Leave off electives that
have no connection. Also, use course names, not numbers
as JOU 3350 doesn't mean anything to hiring managers, but
"Advanced Political Journalism" has clarity in explanation.

- Interests (no one really cares about these unless
they are relevant to the industry- so leave off)

- Quotes and inspirations from others (these have no relevance
to your KSA's so leave it off and save it for the interview)

- Languages (add this to skills and refer to
translation and interpretation specifically)

- References (this should be on a separate sheet;
you'll learn and create this later in this chapter)

The order of information

The research on eye-tracking from The Ladders suggests that clearly marked sections are critical as it has been found that when reviewing job resumes, recruiters spend the most time and focus on job titles. From a purely evidence-based point of view, a hiring manager should be more interested in what you did, rather than where you did it. Meaning, that you want to put the job title first, then the company or organization and location next. In the case of education, the degree comes first, then the school below (see above in Education).

DATES

The dates on a resume should be the least focused on items as they are not keyword specific and can be a point of concern when reviewing your application. Especially in the case of new graduates, the dates on the resume should be out of the immediate F-Zone and should be in a smaller font size (8-9 point) to keep them away from the critical data. If you have many years of experience in an industry, you can make the dates more prominent by raising the point size to 10pt and adding a bold style to the text. But, in all cases, keep the dates to the right of the page, where they are not part of the F-Zone. They can be viewed, but only glanced as eye focus is on the parallel and vertical trails of the F-pattern layout.

For jobs and items in the experience section always
place the job first, then location underneath:
Assistant Manager (JOB TITLE FIRST)   1/2015 - 9/2018
Jones Corporation, Phoenix, AZ. (LOCATION)

STEP FOUR - WRITING YOUR RESUME

Below please review the mission-critical guidelines to follow when writing resume content. These rules will provide grammatical structure and provide some guidelines on writing with confidence.

Write meaningful sentences

Writing the sentences is next. You will fill in the sections with bullets and short KSA-packed sentences. For each section, you are going to need content. Content on the resume comes in the form of KSA's (knowledge, skills, and abilities) with action verbs, keywords, bullets and correct demographic information. Just as we added content to the heading and objective sections, you now must write the bulk of the resume's content. Two things are worth focus here, which are crafting meaningful sentences and the elimination of typos and grammatical errors.

Collect experiences

The most frequently asked questions from students and people I advise on resume construction...What do I write and how much do I need? The answer, write about the things that you did (tasks or decisions) that were important to that project or job and fill up one page. How? Start by thinking about a typical day at work or at one of your experiences. Write down every task you performed in a single day – regardless of how valuable you think they are perceived.

Even every-day responsibilities like sending emails or attending formal or informal meetings with coworkers or supervisors. Then, choose the items that show responsibility, accountability, skills, and trust. See which items match your activities with the jobs you want to apply for to evaluate the potential similarities between what you do and what they do, even if it is not the same exact specific task – that is part of the process of parallel construction. No job or task is too small or meaningless if it requires responsibility, accountability, skills, and trust.

Let's take a retail job, which is a typical bridge job for college and high school students. When deciding what to write, I suggest answering basic questions about their roles, either formal or informal: Are you responsible for handling customers or payments? Did you open or close the store? Doing that well shows that someone trusts you with the most important aspect of their business. As well, were you accountable for helping build and secure sales? If so, you proved that you have sales skills to explain a product line or handle a client transaction. You have to start thinking about what you did and how you can describe it clearly and with value. You must realize that everyone has important qualities that can and should be highlighted on their resume. Don't undersell yourself or forget to give yourself credit for what you have done. That is why you learned how to do research to reflect and collect these experiences and write about them in a meaningful way.

Taking inventory, we can estimate how the resume document may fill out, but we can't be certain because each person has different experiences and holds varied skills, so the sections could be weighted with less or more sentences. As an estimate, expect to write 15-20 sentences for the resume, maximum, per page.

A breakdown of what I see typically from students yields a profile or objective and approximately 5-7 bullets under skills, two - three experience sections with 3-4 bullets each that show the jobs or internships, and an education section with your degrees and possibly additional subheadings to make up for the lack of information in the experience section.

More experienced folks may have a two-page resume that has a longer list of experiences, but regardless, they need to follow the same conventions for the first page so it is flagged as a match. So, this means focus on page one, and then see if page two is even needed.

One way to get the bullet writing process started is by using an "I" to start the sentence and then dropping it for the resume bullet, which is a shortened phrase with a period that does not have any pronouns. I call it the Minus I bullet exercise.

The minus "I" bullet exercise
Start by writing a sentence in first person. Use I, then remove the I and start the sentence with an action verb or a success verb for each sentence.

_____

I managed customer transactions for the electronics department. I grew electronic sales by 20% from 2019-2020.

Now, minus the "I".
• Managed customer transactions for the electronics department. (uses action verb)

_____

I grew sales in my retail division by 10%. (uses success verb) Now, minus the "I".
• Grew sales in my retail division by 10%.

Keep sentences lean
(10-15 WORDS IS PERFECT) Using success verbs is like showing off a high score in a video game. High scores grab attention. The person who sold over $1000 per day, or the professional who closed over 50 accounts in a month portrays success through

sheer use of data points that jump out from the resume.

Maybe you can code a website landing page in minutes, or type 150 words per minute, both attention getting high scores in the digital world, which can be seen as success statements in the resume. Find your high scores in what you have accomplished that can be measured. Sales figures, customers served, money saved, pitches sent, placements acquired, posts created, followers gained, products developed, team accomplishments, and anything measurable qualifies as a high score term for you.

Finally, think about using data points, numerical if available, when creating success verb statements. Reflect on what you have done and analyze how you have contributed to or achieved high scores in your work experiences.

Resume writing guidelines

1 - **Use success verbs** and action verbs together in the active voice (sample: • Evaluated and managed over 100 technical projects for the marketing department. The action verbs are the skills in evaluating and managing. The success verb statement is managed over 100 projects.)

2 - **Embed keywords** into sentences with parallel language (sample: • Ability to develop media lists and create Excel spreadsheets.)

3 - **Use bullets** to create a quick read format (• Wrote over 50 press releases for the new products division, which produced 20 media interviews.)

4 - **Write at least two bullets per job** or section and no more than seven. Less than two bullets add them to another section or delete irrelevant ones from the section if too many.

5 - **Focus on first person usage** in the draft, but eliminate the I's (You do this simply dropping the "I". Wrote press releases for the new products division.)

6 - **Follow a consistent tense** in each section (work, worked) (Work as a manager. Worked as a manager.)

7 - Insert periods at the end of each sentence
(This is a complete sentence.)

8 - Avoid extra-long sentences or super short fragments (No more 20 words per sentence. (10-15 words is ideal)

9 - Describe what you did in your experiences descriptively. (It's OK to use some industry jargon here, but don't use abbreviations)

10 - Avoid fluff and don't lie. Don't include sentences that are not truthful or are directed at the qualities everyone should have. For example, describing yourself as dedicated and hardworking – this is literally expected in everyone, so it doesn't need to be in the resume.

11 - Edit and revise the resume twice (at least). You should do this to insure layout, flow, clarity, and correctness. Get a fresh eye if needed (someone else) The resume is not complete until you have looked at it at least three separate times to flesh out all clumsy sentences and errors.

Adding dates to the resume

The dates that are listed on the resume for each job, degree, certification, or experience should be accurate and precise. You should put items in the form of months or years and be ready to have these dates checked. In cases where your job title changed, say you were promoted for example, at the same location, and then you should add each title to the same section but add the proper dates for each job title. Dates should be to the far right of each section. This is especially true for new graduates who have little experience or mainly three-month blocks at internships. Dates do not need to be large in font size – 8 pt. in okay, especially if you have gaps or are a new graduate. The dates sit outside of the F-Zone primarily so that they are not focused on during a human scan.

The final line of the resume is optional, but recommended if there is space: References and portfolio available upon request. If you don't have a professional portfolio of work in either a print book or website, leave the whole sentence off. No need to place "references available upon request" alone as it will be expected that you will submit them before the final hiring process is complete.

Editing and revising the resume

The resume editing process is as important as the first draft; maybe even more so because it is where you apply the polish by removing the clutter and amplifying the voice with action. The importance of editing and revision of the resume cannot be overstated.

Good editing is good writing. To create a great resume alone, as most folks do, you need to take on two roles, that of the writer and of the editor. You have to write the resume as the writer and then walk away. Come back to it as an editor, and put yourself in the position of the person reading it. A useful method for editing is to print out your resume on paper and then mark it up with a red pen. This will help you catch the same errors that a hiring manager might see. It will also help you work through the editing process with greater care. Once you make the marks, go back to your digital document and make the changes, crossing off each one on the hard copy as you make the fixes electronically.

Finally, you can make edits to your document and then print it out again to compare it to the marked up version and see how it has been improved or if it needs more attention.

To edit on paper, you can use these simple marks

Mary Smith

Brooklyn, NY
671-000-000
msmith@gmail.com
www.marysmith.com

Objective

Seeking to apply my skills, experience, and passion in public relations and marketing to a growing organization in the fashion & apparel industry.

Skills

- Proficiency in Adobe Photoshop, Microsoft Office, and social media platforms.
- Strategizing and scheduling social media content.
- Ability to maintain archives, samples, and showroom pieces including sample tracking.

Experience

Editorial Public Relations Intern *January 2020 – Present*
Brooks Brothers, New York, NY
- Monitored daily press mentions in print and digital placements.
- Maintained sample closet for stylist pulls, press requests, and studio pulls.
- Conducted research for influencer collaborations and new talent to dress.

Public Relations & Marketing Temp *August 2018 – December 2019*
Alexis Bittar, Brooklyn, NY
- Created and scheduled content on social media platforms while interacting with followers to maintain brand's social presence.
- Responsible for archive collection of jewelry i.e. sample tracking.
- Assisted in strategizing and executing influencer/media gifting programs.

Human Resources Intern *June 2019 – August 2019*
Fresh (LVMH), New York, NY
- Created and maintained brand's digital presence on LinkedIn.
- Implemented precise content calendar inclusive of company events, LVMH happenings, and original content ideas.
- Responsible for regular upkeep and posting to LinkedIn, keeping content relevant and followers engaged.

Sales & Operations Assistant *December 2018 – Present*
Versace 5th Avenue, New York, NY
- Served as brand ambassador, developing strong relationships with clients.
- Kept up-to-date on current product knowledge including pricing and promotions.
- Provided superior customer service, placing great importance on brand experience and storytelling.

Education

Bachelor of Science in Advertising Communications *May 2020*
St. John's University, NY
- Minor in International Studies, Concentration in Fashion
- St. John's University – Rome, Italy (Spring 2018)

References and portfolio available upon request.

FIGURE 4-10: Edited resume example.

VOICE, TENSE, AND CLUTTER

The three main problems that I see when editing resumes are grammar issues that include use of the passive voice, incorrect tense, and the overuse of phrases with the same page of sentences. Collectively, voice, tense, and clutter are the areas that you need to focus on when editing.

Voice

The voice of a sentence focuses on who or what (the subject) gives the action (active verb). Active verbs are defined by the subject giving the action directly, whereas passive verbs get disconnected from the subject with auxiliary verbs or are just in the wrong place in the sentence. When writing and editing resume bullets, you are looking to eliminate passive sentences that use auxiliary verbs such as was, have been, and is being. Prepositions also create passive sentences with words like for, to, and in that yield sentence clutter. These grammar tightening issues pop up more frequently when writing cover letters, but we should be caring and focused on every sentence in the resume to make it clear and captive by rooting out passive writing.

Here are some passive sentence editing examples:
- Have been processing insurance claims for the past two years as an adjuster. (Passive)
- Processed insurance claims as an adjuster for the past two years (Active)

- Was performing studies and reporting qualitative and quantitative marketing research. (Passive)
- Performed studies reporting qualitative and quantitative marketing research. (Active)

Tense

As writers, we must pay attention to time, and how we represent it in our sentences. If we get confused in our use of tenses, the reader becomes confused. Therefore, we cannot get lazy with tenses and must remember that anything in the present tense should be first in our experience sections, with past tense sections coming further on the page in the chronology. The tenses in each section should match each other.

Checking tenses is not difficult if you simplify the usages by

applying only present and past tenses to your bullet sentences:
The present has no "ed" at the end.
The past has "ed" at the end.
Don't use "ing" on the end of a verb, stay
with past or present tense.

For your current job: Remove "ed" from all action verbs
Current:
• Perform studies and report qualitative and
quantitative marketing research. (present tense)

Past job: Add "ed" to action verbs
• Performed 100 studies and reported qualitative and
quantitative marketing research. (past tense)

Avoid progressive tenses in sentences that use "ing" verbs and
the linking verbs was and were as they add clutter. In addition,
stay away not use the perfect tense (has and had) as it also adds
words that bloat sentences that don't need expanded prose.

Clutter

Writing is a sloppy process when we draft. We need to edit
the words and sentences in the resume carefully, to trim the
wasted words. If we don't comb through the words and reduce
the clutter, it becomes difficult to understand the thought
behind the text. Editing out clutter is an important step in
polishing the resume and achieving the best use of space and
language. By deleting pesky words that get between subjects
and verbs, you reduce clutter and project in the active voice.

Resume editing checklist

What are you looking for when editing your resume? We have outlined items to seek out during editing sessions.

1 - Spelling errors – which are obvious but often overlooked.

2 - "I"'s in the bullets points – remove all pronouns from bullets.

3 - Repetitive action verbs – spread out the action verbs and remove line after line duplicates.

4 - Inconsistent and incorrect tenses – anything in the past should be written in the past tense such as work vs. worked. Don't use "ing" verbs with the progressive tense.

5 - Incorrect spacing or too many pages – use one space after a period, and limit your resume to one or two full pages, maximum. Never have a resume 1.5 page resume.

6 - Missing periods at the end of sentences – Sentences with bullets get periods and headings do not.

7 - More than one font or ornate fonts – Arial is best, keep it to a single standard font.

8 - Prepositions that clutter writing – eliminate these small words: for, to, and in.

9 - Auxiliary verbs that veil the active voice – eliminate was, have been, and is being.

10 - Lack of action verbs, keywords, and relevant success sentences – revise words to align parallel language with job descriptions.

Intelligence resume template

The resume sample is available in both Google Docs and Microsoft Word formats for download in the Resources section.

The template files contain embedded style sheets and spacing. Simply type over the text with your information and save as a Word document, Google Doc, or PDF. A one-page format is available and can be saved as a new document, then updated with your profile, skills, experience, and education for the second page.

Marilyn Smith

2 Half Hollow Place
Niagara, NY 00000
671-000-0000
msmith@mail.com
marilynsmith.portfoliovillage.com

Profile

Dedicated and accomplished professional in the field of marketing. Successful digital media and communications specialist for the past two years working in event management. Seeking to utilize my skills and experience in marketing management to help a flourishing organization.

Skills

- Ability to perform typography using InDesign.
- Experience producing press materials using MS Word.
- Proficient in developing presentations using MS Powerpoint.
- Fluent in the use of research tools including databases, search engines, and indexes.
- Ability to write corporate communications materials.

Experience

Assistant Events Coordinator

January 2008– Present

West Coast Saloons, Madison, NY
- Responsible for building client databases via phone and email.
- Assisted in booking private parties and events.
- Served clients in a fast-paced setting.
- Handled large monetary sums and closed cash registers.

Account Coordinator

March 2006– August 2007

Freshbrick–, Inc., Madison, NY
- Personal assistant to two agency owners.
- Responsible for providing support on all projects including product launches, political campaigns, fundraisers, and trade fairs.
- Performed daily clerical duties including bookkeeping and phone calls.

Cheerleading Coach

March 2006– August 2007

Massachusetts Public Schools, Manorville, MA
- Trained and coached athletes in cheerleading ranging from ages 12 – 18.
- Responsible for oversight and management of the financial budget for sports programs.
- Organized local competitions and met fundraising goals.

Education

Bachelor of Science in Mass Communications

May 2009

Niagara University, NY
- Dean's List
- Varsity Cheerleading Team Scholarship

Associate in Science in Liberal Arts

May 2007

Niagara County Community College, NY

References and portfolio available upon request.

FIGURE 4-11: The final intelligence resume template.

Creating your reference sheet

The reference sheet is an essential piece for the resume package. It doesn't need to be submitted immediately, but you need to have it available on request. You should list three references maximum and no fewer than two. Make sure that you contact each reference in advance and ask if they would feel comfortable providing a positive reference for you, and if it is okay to list their contact information.

Keep it consistent looking with the same resume and cover letter fonts and spacing.

The design of the reference sheet uses the same heading font size and style as the resume and the cover letter. Copy the heading from your resume and paste it into your reference sheet and cover letter. Or, use the "save as" command to save out a new file. Leave the name heading alone and delete the resume text. Then add the references below your name heading.

Marilyn Smith

2 Half Hollow Place
Niagara, NY 00000
671-000-0000
msmith@mail.com
marilynsmith.portfoliovillage.com

References

Anthony Smith
President
West Coast Saloons, Madison, NY
E: adsmith@wcs.com
Tel: 555-121-1233

Bella Hughes
Marketing Manager
FreshClick, Madison, NY
E: bhughes@freshclickstore.com
Tel: 333-212-5789

Karla Jackson
Athletic Director
Manor Schools, Evandale, NY
E: karla.jackson@mscsx.edu
Tel: 555-1212-123

FIGURE 4-12: The reference sheet uses the same style sheet as the resume.

Saving and submitting your resume

You'll need three electronic documents prepared when you submit your resume to jobs on the Internet. ATS systems accepting your resume typically request Word documents saved as either .doc or .docx. Some systems also collect PDF documents so be ready with both.

SAVING AS A WORD DOC

If you use another word processing program, you'll need to save as a .Word document. The .doc format allows the ATS software to scan the text for keyword criteria. It also makes it easy to copy and paste the resume text into a field box if needed, while still maintaining the structure and formatting.

CREATING A PDF

Another file format that may be requested in job applications is Adobe Acrobat portable document format, which is a .PDF. You can save out a .PDF using the SAVE AS command in Microsoft Word and choosing .PDF from the menu or this can be done in Google Docs. The .PDF file can also be output from other software applications using the FILE EXPORT command. Be prepared for online submissions with both .doc and .pdf files.

EXERCISE (4A) - WRITE AND DESIGN THE RESUME

Now that you have learned how to create the resume, you can begin to write and design your resume and reference sheet.

Next chapter: Cover letter

Now that you have a resume ready, you will create a cover letter that will pitch you to a potential employer and reference your knowledge, skills, and abilities in a professional narrative.

Notes

Chapter 5.

COVER LETTER
Get to the point and persuade.

Chapter objectives
- Understand the purpose of the cover letter
- Connect your research with your cover letter
- Utilize keywords and parallel language in the cover letter
- Understand the style, length and format of the cover letter
- Write an engaging, action oriented three paragraph cover letter
- Develop a clean, clutter-free cover letter design

The purpose of the cover letter
The cover letter is essentially a pitch letter. A pitch letter is a common tool for public relations specialists who work in media relations. In PR, pitch letters are used to pitch a story or an interview to an editor, reporter, producer, or other media decision maker. The goal is to get publicity in the form of a media placement or interview. The pitch letter is short, fact based, and focused on a particular audience, meaning the letter directly relates to what the media person is looking for his or her audience. The cover letter does the same thing; it presents you as the story and asks for further action in the form of a resume review and ultimately an interview. The cover letter gets the resume looked at by the decision maker. So, it's important that we give them what they are looking for in a candidate immediately. There's no time for fluff.

Cover letter strategy - persuasion
In order to be persuasive, you must lead the reader in the right direction. You want the reader to act positively and read the resume. The reader could be a Human Resources Manager, a department head, a head hunter, an executive or principal of the company, or a potential internship site manager. You want to cater the cover letter to the industry and opportunities so be specific in what you write and how you write it.

Include these important items in the cover letter to be persuasive:

- Include the keywords that appear in the ad or job description

- Include clarification that you understand what the

hiring person is looking for in a candidate.

- Include snippets from your resume that illustrate your skills and experience.

- Include an offer to present your professional portfolio of work, either in print or online.

- Include a request to interview, but not directly (see paragraph three).

Cover letter structure and format

The cover letter can be written many different ways. There are various opinions handed down by all those who give advice on this subject. My idea is always to make it simple, direct, and persuasive. The way you do that is to get to the point right away and be focused on connecting what you did with what the job opportunity is requiring. You need to show that you are a match, right from the start. You need a specific job opportunity and description to craft the keywords and experience. You may also need to go back to the job, industry, and skills research you did previously to find other important items you may need to include in the cover letter (the intangibles).
I believe that simple is the new fancy. To achieve simple is not to skimp on value, but to provide clarity, which yields an abundance of information. With this in mind, I offer a simple structure for the cover letter. My "default" cover letter is three paragraphs. That's it. If you can master writing these three paragraphs, you will be able to quickly and effectively write cover letters for the rest of your career.

Start with your heading - this will be the same as the one used on the resume. Then, two spaces and list the job posting information.

Add the date
then the job posting
RE: The _____ position (job # XYZ)

then
The Greeting:
Dear _____,
Always address the cover letter to a specific person. If you don't have a name, address it

Dear Hiring Manager,

or

Dear Human Resources Manager.

Do not use " To Whom it May Concern", it's too impersonal. You can always search the company website or make a call to research out the name of who will be receiving the resumes.

The lead paragraph (first) The Keyword paragraph
This paragraph is critical to getting the attention of the human resources screener who is looking for the important keywords. You must identify what they are looking for and then tell them that you have it. Finally, indicate the specific job and if asked, give your salary requirements or professional rates.

"To be an effective _____ , one must possess skills and abilities in _____, _____, and _____. I have these qualities and have practiced them for the past _____years at _____. If _____ needs a dedicated professional in the field of _____, then please accept my application for the position of _____."(I am seeking compensation of _____ per year.)

The beefy middle paragraph (second)
The Experience Paragraph
This is where you expand on what you have written in the resume. This can be one-two paragraphs if needed, but try to keep it to one. You want to this to be concrete, and not fluff. Make sure to expand on what you list in your resume. Be specific and try to offer results or experiences that highlight your performance and what you learned or gained. This really ignites the juices of hiring managers.

Here's an example that could be used for a new graduate...

"The enclosed resume highlights my experience and abilities in _____ and _____. During my internship at _____, I was able to build a library of 500 media clips and secure 25 interviews for national authors including _____. This experience propelled me to secure another internship at _____. At this job, I worked with creative teams to plan and execute charity events for several clients including _____, which yielded over $25k in donations. In addition, my part time job at _____ demands impeccable customer service and has driven me to earn employee awards for in-store professionalism.

The closing paragraph (third) The Action Paragraph
This is where you end the conversation and ask for action. You want the person reading your resume or pass it along to the next decision maker in the hiring process. You want to ask for the interview and offer to present your portfolio.

"I would appreciate the opportunity to present my portfolio and discuss how my skills and experience can benefit _____. Thank you for your consideration. I look forward to your reply."

Sincerely, (or you can use Respectfully)
(sign here)
Your full name

William Hopkins II

1234 Lost Path Drive 2nd floor
Anywhere, NY 11555
email@gmail.com
Website address

Mr. Martin Maze
CEO Intent Communications
100000 Madison Ave. Suite 600
New York, NY 10017
212-000-0000

May 1, 2012

Dear Mr. Maze,

To be an effective assistant account executive, a professional must have skills and experience in writing, verbal communication, and leadership. I have those qualities and have practiced them as an intern for Internet Communications and as a Director of Media Affairs for the Warming Hearts Society at my university. If INTENT Communications needs a dedicated specialist, please consider my application for the position of assistant account executive. I am seeking compensation of $40,000 annually.

The enclosed resume highlights my experiences with financial and micro financial public relations and non-profit marketing. While working for GLOBE, the not-for-profit micro financial institution within the St. John's Community, I was able to raise $2,000 within three months and create a lifelong network of donors for the student run organization. Working on the marketing team, we accomplished these planned goals by producing a water bottle promotion and then sold the product at over 25 external events. I used my applied knowledge of social media and how it is used in financial communications to develop a database of reporter's social media accounts and created an application to compare them, which streamlined the process for reaching out to reporters online. The project created collateral for current and future clients and generated additional billable hours. As the Director of Media Affairs for the Warming Hearts Society, I was responsible for establishing media contacts, branding a coherent and concise organizational image and pitching media contacts about events. These work experiences have allowed me to build and exercise an array of technical and persuasive skills.

I would appreciate the opportunity to discuss your organization's needs and present samples of my work. Thank you for your consideration. I look forward to your reply.

Sincerely,

William Hopkins II

FIGURE 5-1 Sample cover letter

Cover letter editing and revision

After writing the cover letter using the template, walk away from it for a while. Go back to it and act as an editor. − Ask these critical questions:

1. Does this letter flow? Read it out loud to make sure that you don't have extensive sentences - nothing longer than one line. Check the beefy paragraph.

2. Next, check the sentences for grammar and spelling errors. Look at tense, clutter, and levels of keywords, and success verbs.

3. Then, make sure that the content is punchy and results driven. Did you present achievements and contributions to the company or organization? Are you explaining what you did in concrete terms? Have you shown "results" with statistics or outcomes?

4. Did you address the letter to the contact person? Did you respectfully ask for action in the last paragraph? Is your heading contact information correct and up to date?

5. Is the cover letter consistently formatted? Is the heading the same as the resume? Are the fonts and spacing consistent throughout?

Style and design

You want the style and design to match the resume and reference sheet exactly. The heading should be the same, the font size and styles should match, and the spacing should be the same. Make sure that you follow the standard design format with consistent headings using a uniform style sheet.

EXERCISE (5A): WRITE AND DESIGN THE COVER LETTER.
Now that you have learned how to create the cover letter using the three paragraph format, you can begin to write and design your professional cover letter.

Next chapter: Portfolio book

You now have a resume and cover letter to establish a sound set of career communication to help you promote yourself and career. Next, you'll create the portfolio book to establish a source of evidence that shows off your knowledge, skills, and abilities (KSA's).

Notes

Chapter 6.

PORTFOLIO BOOK
Present your evidence.

Chapter objectives
- Understand the purpose of the print portfolio book
- Create a portfolio content list and outline
- Gather and format your portfolio content
- Understand the style, length and format of the e-portfolio book
- Build an effective print portfolio book

Print portfolio overview
A portfolio is a platform and collection of tangible evidence that represents a person's professional identity. The print portfolio is a tool for you to show off your professional work. It pitches your abilities, such as a brochure would and with real evidence. The portfolio book is powerful because it is the most accessible, impressive persuasion tool you have beyond yourself. It provides a hiring manager, prospective client, or organization the ability to closely view your professional work, projects, and writing. The print portfolio can contain all types of content, from writing samples, to visual design pieces, photos, and even screenshots of web pages, animations, and broadcast work. You can present these materials in a neat, organized, self-made portfolio book. Portfolio books can be used across disciplines and majors. The ability to create your own print portfolio is an important career communication skill as employers start to require evidence of abilities beyond the resume.

Why use a print portfolio?
- It provides tangible evidence of your skills and experience.
- It sets you above other applicants who have no portfolio.
- It allows you to connect with your own work and will help you talk about it in an interview.
- It gives you confidence because it is a self promotional tool that can do the talking for you.

How to use a print portfolio
- You can show it during a job interview.
- You can leave it behind after a job interview.
- You can use it to secure freelance jobs.

E-Portfolio usage

You can convert your print portfolio document to a PDF and email it to a hiring manager. The converted PDF file is known as an E-portfolio (electronic portfolio - a portfolio based on an electronic file). Different than a bunch of files, the portfolio has a structure, style, and your personal brand as a consistent element.

Creating the print portfolio book

You can create the print portfolio book without having extensive digital design skills. I have helped hundreds of students create portfolio books. The book can be easily assembled using MS Word or MS PowerPoint, or Google Docs or Slides. You can design each single page, then spiral bind the pages, which makes the production process inexpensive and simple. I have taught hundreds of students and job seekers from many fields and disciplines how to create portfolio books. Now, I'll show you how to create your own.

Steps:

Step one: Portfolio book format and setup
Step two: Reflect and collect work
Step three: Design your pages
Step four: Edit and revise
Step five: Portfolio book finishing

Format and Setup

There are two typical formats for the print portfolio book: portrait or landscape. You can create the book either of these ways but there are some suggested guidelines for which one to use depending upon your work and graphic art skill level. Portrait portfolio book layout is straight up letter size paper (8.5 x 11) with the binding on the long edge. It is the most common size and the easiest to layout, especially if there are many single page writing pieces such as essays, fliers, or press releases. I recommend this layout if you have a large group of writing samples or just want the easiest format. Landscape portfolio book layout is letter size paper (8.5 x 11) with the binding on the short edge (or long edge for a "flip book"). This layout is a bit more complicated to execute because it requires scaling of most elements and less page space to work with. This layout works well for graphically heavy portfolios for art, photography, graphic design, or advertising.

Key Points to remember about the portfolio book setup
- The portfolio book needs space for binding, so keep at
  least a 1-1.5 inch margin on the edge to be bound.

- The portfolio book does not need page numbers
  because it is short. This will allow you to remove pages
  or shuffle pages around and rebind if needed.

- The portfolio book should be consistent in fonts, placement
  of captions, logos, and case study headings.

- Try to place elements according to a visual grid.

- The portfolio book should have a cover and a contact page.

- The portfolio book pages can be one sided or double sided.

- The portfolio book should be at least 5
  pages and no more than 15 pages.

Now, it's your turn...
Choose a portfolio book layout style: portrait or landscape.

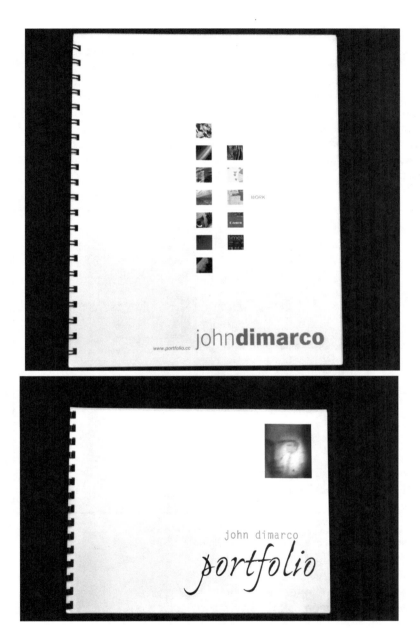

FIGURE 6-1 Print portfolio layouts: portrait (top) and landscape.

Portfolio book structure

Every publication has a structure. Your portfolio book should have a consistent structure that you follow when you layout the pages. There are a host of variations on the layout, but you will have three to four consistent items on the interior pages at most times. These include a page header, the actual work sample (text or graphics), the caption or case study, and the personal logo or page background. These items will balance out your book and provide a greater level of clarity and professionalism. Captions and case studies help explain written or intricate work. Elements such as the logo will reinforce your personal brand.

Museum Poster Design

Problem: Create a museum poster for the Metropolitan Museum of Art based on an original photograph.

Solution: Designed a poster using text and color matching while placing it in different environments.

Tools: Photoshop

Role: Graphic Designer

FIGURE 6-2 Print portfolio page items include captions, creative work, and personal logos in a printed and bound book.

Make a tentative decision...
Choose the structure items that you initially plan to include: header, caption or case study, personal logo. You must have the actual work samples.

Reflect and Collect

Now you will reflect on your experiences and begin to collect the evidence you need to show that you have certain knowledge, skills and abilities that make you a match for a potential job.

Portfolio book length

As mentioned above, the portfolio book needs to be long enough to show your work and skills, but not too long that it becomes difficult to look through. The ideal length in my opinion is somewhere between, 12-15 pages. This gives you enough length to show eight or nine work samples and include separator pages or pages with case studies. The best way to determine the length of the book is to create the laundry list and then a content outline, which we will tackle next.

Print portfolio content decisions

What content should be included in the print portfolio? It depends on your area of expertise. Some jobs require certain work samples, such as public relations, which demands that portfolios have writing samples. Or advertising, which asks for creative work You will need to reflect on what you have done in the past and collect the work (artifacts) so that you can present it in the print portfolio book. Aim to place work that relates to the job your are currently looking to secure.

Answer this question:

My print portfolio promotes me as a _____.
Place the most relevant content into your portfolio book that promotes you in that role. Don't try to put in everything that you have ever done, but only the best, most relevant things that you have done.

Here are some suggestions for print portfolio content:
- Personal photo
- Project samples
- Writing samples
- Blog writing samples
- Social media page samples
- Student project work
- Art and design work
- Photos
- Professional activities

- Presentations
- Event materials and photos
- Volunteer work
- Project case studies
- Animations (as screenshots)
- Video clips (as screenshots)
- Illustrations
- Digital Images
- Educational philosophy
- Professional Goals
- Personal Mission Quote
- Research reports/papers
- Lesson plans (teachers)
- Anything else that is truly relevant and you can digitize

Content list and outline

The content list compiles the materials that you would like to put in the print portfolio in no particular order. The main thing here is to be specific in your descriptions of work so that you can identify the file during production. And second, the most important part of this process is to be able to collect a sample of the work in digital form. Or, you can you shoot a picture or scan the work to get it into the portfolio book. Without the digital file, you can't show the work in the book. If this is not possible you should cross the work off the content list.

EXERCISE (6A) - CONTENT LIST

Create the content list of potential work (be specific in naming each work - for example: "Coat Drive press release" or "homeless charity event photo -2021"). Don't use a generic name like "photo one"

Write the content outline and section headings

The content outline is a list of all the materials that you would like to put in the print portfolio in order with headings. It marries the "sections" with the "samples". This is where you establish your book sections and add projects from the laundry list you created earlier. Sections should consist of major areas that you have sample work for. These can be broad categories such as "writing", which could have a variety of writing samples, or they can be a narrow category like "press releases". It depends on how many pieces you have and what the industry is that you are promoting yourself in is looking for. Look to the keywords you researched to get some suggested headings.

Section headings need to have at least two work samples in them. If you have at least two or more pieces to show, you have a potential section. With only one piece, you may not want to create a separate section in the portfolio book; rather, you could add the work into another section or maybe even eliminate it.

You can also be proactive and create sample pieces on your own and add them to the sections (create a flier for a fictitious event or a mock press release for example). Later on, you can use the section headings as navigation headings for your Web portfolio. You might think of other work that you have not yet completed but plan to put into the portfolio in the future (as in the case of working on this during a school semester). You can leave a placeholder page in the book dummy but keep it out of the final printed work.

EXERCISE (6B) - CONTENT OUTLINE
Create the content outline with portfolio book sections. List the headings and then add the content from the list under the appropriate sections.

Make the DUMMY Portfolio Book
The best way to figure out how the page will layout and look is to create a "dummy" portfolio book. The dummy book will have rough sketched layouts that show placement of images, headings, caption or case studies, and personal logos. You should create each page that will be in the portfolio book and list the sample work that will go on each page. This way, when you are laying out your book, you will be able to have a clear path during production and can easily make pre-production edits by swapping and switching pages around in the dummy.

FIGURE 6-3 Dummy portfolio page example. The dummy is used for content and structure planning. Sketch the pages using simple to understand symbols. Use thick lines for headings, boxes for content, lines for text and circles for logos.

EXERCISE (6C) - CREATE THE DUMMY
Make the dummy portfolio. Take 20 single sheets of 8.5 x 11 paper. Then use these sketching symbols to position the page elements. No need to draw out the images, this document is "for placement only" (FPO)

Prepare digital work for placement in the book layout
To be placed in a book, work must be digitized, which means being converted to digital form. There are two kinds of content format for the print portfolio book: text and images. Text based work can be copied and pasted or typed directly into the page layout program you use. Graphics will need to be inserted (or placed) into the document page alongside text. Before you insert images in the book layout make sure that they are digitized and are high resolution at least 266 -300 ppi (pixels per inch).

If you scan, 266-300 dpi to size is a good target for images that will be printed at the highest resolutions on a laser or inkjet printer. Use high resolution settings on your digital camera if you are taking photos of work or events that will be published in the portfolio book. This will insure the highest quality output available on the printer. You can use any file format that your page layout program accepts, but you may want to stick to .PNG., TIF or .JPG (TIFF or JPEG). These formats print on desktop printers.

If you use screenshots of your work, be aware that they are low resolution (96 or 72 dpi). They will print OK at 100% on a desktop printer, but not great. Always take screenshots on the largest monitor available, and avoid laptops for that task.

Get organized - Make your folders
You need to get your files organized. To do this, go to your desktop or documents folder and create a folder titled " PORTFOLIO 20XX" (add the year).

Then, inside, create two folders:
"HIGH RES-PRINT" and "LOW RES - WEB". You will place all the high res (266-300 dpi) images for the print book in the HIGH RES folder. Later on, when you develop your Web portfolio, you will convert the high res files into low res (72 PPI) before uploading them if you want to get the most performance and file storage out of your Website.

The digital toolbox
Having the right tools allow you to do the job successfully. Building a portfolio, whether it is printed or online, requires the use of digital tools and technology. Now using these tools can be simplified and boiled down so that most everyone can complete their portfolio book. Most people have experience with MS Word, PowerPoint, or Google Docs, so they are good tools to use for basic page layout.

Some people have experience with digital design programs such as Adobe InDesign or Adobe Illustrator – they may want to use higher end software to complete their book. That's fine too. Besides a page layout program, you will most likely need an image editing program to save digital images to other formats or to crop or edit images. The tools don't really matter, what matters is that you have a tool set to use during this process.

Here's what you will need:
COMPUTER: Mac or Windows

PAGE LAYOUT SOFTWARE: MS Word, PowerPoint or Google Docs or Slides work great. You can also create pages using Canva or Photoshop.

IMAGE EDITING SOFTWARE: This is optional if all your work is digital and in .PNG, .TIF or .JPG file format. If so, you can import the images into the page layout program and resize the image. You may need Adobe Photoshop or another image editing program (Apple Preview allows resizing also) for creating converting graphics to PDF for insertion into your page layout program.

Taking screenshots
Many times you need to take a picture of the screen to get a digital copy of your work so that it can be printed. This especially needed with Website pages, social media pages, animations, videos, and commercials. A screenshot is a copy of the screen that gets pasted to the clipboard (Windows) or saved to your desktop (Mac) as a bitmap file. The screenshot is 72 (Mac) or 96 dpi (Win) and will be the same pixel size as your screen size or whever you grab (1920 x 1080 for example). The higher the screen resolution size the larger the screenshot size. So taking screenshots on larger monitors with high resolution is best, rather than using laptop screens.

TO TAKE A SCREENSHOT:
MAC: Apple + Shift 3
- Takes a shot of the entire screen and PNG files for each shot are placed on the page as "Picture1.png, Picture2.png, etc. These images will need to be cropped to show only the image and not the background desktop or menus.
MAC Apple + Shift 4

- Creates cross hairs on the screen and allows you to drag over what you want to copy. Then, PNG files for each shot are placed on the page as "Picture1.png, Picture2.png, etc. On Windows computers you can use the "Print screen" key, which copies the entire screen to the clipboard. The clipboard can be pasted into a document (CTRL + V). Keep in mind that clipboard images are low resolution (72 or 96 dpi).

Begin to collect the digital pieces you need to place inside of the portfolio book. Place the files in your high resolution folder (Hi RES Print) and continue to add as you discover and create new work.

Page layout
You have many options when it comes to page layouts in the portfolio book. You must make design decisions on where the structure items will go on the page. Placement of the heading, caption, personal logo and sample work must have visual harmony and consistency.

Before you add your work, you should create a NEW DOCUMENT in your page layout program. This will be your receptacle document and it will become your final print portfolio book.

In MS Word or Google Docs or Slides, you will be inserting text boxes and image boxes, and then populating them with your work samples. Use boxes instead of in-line text and graphics because it allows you to position the text and graphical elements freely on the page. This emulates the same method used in professional page layout programs including Adobe InDesign.

Design your pages
You can showcase all types of work in your print portfolio. Anything can be represented and explained including text documents, artwork, animations, videos, photographs, advertisements, and so on. You should use the content outline as a guide when managing your book content. The way you lay out the work on the page depends on the type of work. For instance, video work or motion graphics may be smaller on the page, but presented as multiple images, while advertisements or fliers would be larger on the page to show greater detail or copy. Regardless of work, quality and consistency are critical across the board. The work needs to be well done and relevant, but also remember that production value is equally important.

EXERCISE (6E) - CREATE YOUR PORTFOLIO BOOK DRAFT
Use Google docs or MS Word or PowerPoint to begin to create your portfolio book pages in draft form. You'll edit and add work as you go through the process of refinement

Portfolio book layout steps

This lesson shows how to use Google Docs to make your portfolio book. You should have your PORTFOLIO files located in one folder. – DRAG that folder on to your Google drive for easy placement in the GOOGLE PRINT portfolio.

FIGURE 6-4 (Below) How to build a portfolio in Google Docs

1. Setup Your Free Google Account.

You'll need to have a Google account to use Google sites. Create one at Google.com for free.

2. Launch Google Drive to acess tools

Go to www.Google.com and click on the menu next to your name and click DRIVE

3. CREATE A NEW DOCUMENT
Select the + and then click > GOOGLE
DOCS > New Blank document.

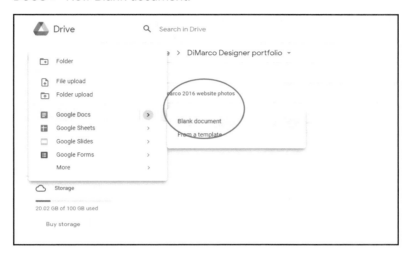

4. INSERT AN IMAGE
Select the INSERT MENU click > INSERT IMAGE > Click
on DRIVE or UPLOAD to insert a portfolio image.

5. SET IMAGE OPTIONS - wrap and position

Click the image and Select the : MENU and click > ALL IMAGE
OPTIONS > Click on TEXT WRAPPING and set to BEHIND TEXT.
--- To move the image on the page fluidly:
Click the image and Select POSITION from the Image
Option Panel. Click the FIX POSITION ON PAGE button.

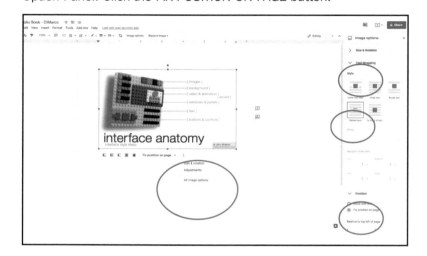

6. INSERT A TEXT BOX CAPTION

Select the INSERT MENU click > INSERT DRAWING > Click
on NEW to insert a new text box that can be fluidly moved.

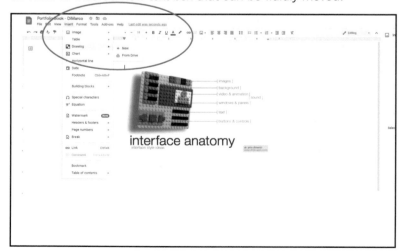

7. TYPE YOUR CAPTION and FORMAT

From the DRAWING WINDOW click > INSERT TEXT BOX
icon > DRAG THE BOX > Type the caption and set the
size font and color > Click SAVE AND CLOSE.

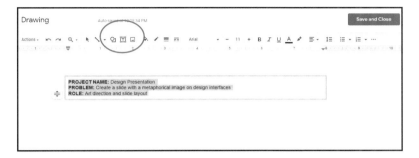

8. SET TEXT BOX OPTIONS - Wrap and position

Click the text box and Select the : MENU and click > ALL IMAGE
OPTIONS > Click on TEXT WRAPPING and set to IN FRONT OF TEXT.
--- To move the text box on the page fluidly:
Click the box and Select POSITION from the Image Option
Panel. Click the FIX POSITION ON PAGE button.

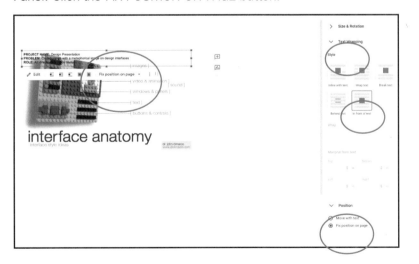

9. INSERT THE PERSONAL LOGO

Select the INSERT MENU click > INSERT IMAGE > Click on DRIVE or UPLOAD to insert a personal logo file. SET IMAGE OPTIONS - TEXT WRAP and POSITION - as you did in STEP 5.

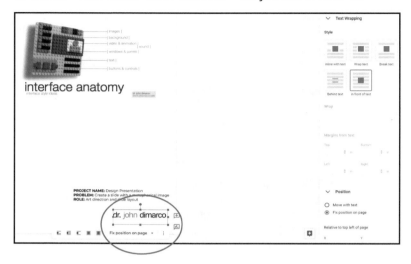

10. REVIEW THE NEW PORTFOLIO PAGE

Make any edits to pages as needed before printing or saving to .PDF format.

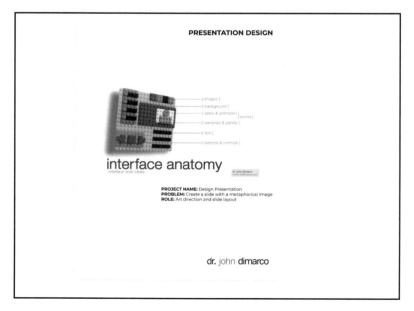

Portfolio book production goals

Here are five production goals to achieve when showcasing work in the portfolio book. This also applies to the Web portfolio. The person viewing the portfolio will be happier and more receptive to your work.

1. Insure all images are crisp and clear. No one likes to look at blurry, pixelated images.

2. Each piece of work has a caption or case study that explains it and your role. No one likes to be guessing when they are evaluating someone else's work.

3. Make all the work consistent in size and placement - watch the binding space. No one likes to strain their eyes with detailed images that are too small or be visually overwhelmed by images that are too big. Make sure nothing is cut off or runs into the binding.

4. Categorize work appropriately and start the portfolio book with the best, most relevant material. No one likes to waste time reviewing a portfolio book that has no relevant evidence.

5. Finish the book properly with a strong, professional binding. No one like pages to fall out of a book. Everyone likes quality.

Portfolio book content strategies

You'll need to decide what goes in to the portfolio – your content decisions are vital to making the book fit your needs and showcasing your evidence of KSA's.

Showcasing textual (written) work

Written work is very common to have. If you are not a designer or an artist, much of your work may be text-based. You may have academic work like papers, essays, poems, or articles. Maybe you possess professional work like press releases, lesson plans, social posts, and stories. Many graduating students and professionals have some balance of both. Written work can be represented as text or a graphic in the print portfolio.

As text, you would open the original document in a program such as Microsoft Word or Google Docs. From there, you can save the document as .PDF and place it back into the portfolio as a graphic. By doing this, the formatting and graphics in the document stay in tact and can placed and scaled in the portfolio book. Or, you can work within the document and make a new portfolio page, then copy and paste the work into the new portfolio book. This allows you to edit the work if needed and manipulate the size and spacing of the text and paragraphs.

In cases of multiple page work, present an excerpt, a notable one page sample of the work, and provide the line "full work available upon request" or provide a URL reference or QR code to an online sample at the bottom of the page. Make sure that you have a caption or a case study to explain the work, especially because it is in partial form.

Scanning or Exporting as PDF
Another way to represent the text document in the portfolio is as an image. You can scan or photograph a text document (an essay, for example). But in most cases, it won't be great quality in the book if the source document was a desktop print. The text will not be very sharp unless it is scanned or shot at very high resolution and the image is cleaned up in Adobe Photoshop. So, I only recommend it as a last resort. It is better to save the document as a PDF out of the program it was created in, if possible, as this will bring in a high resolution version that will be sharp at scaled sizes.

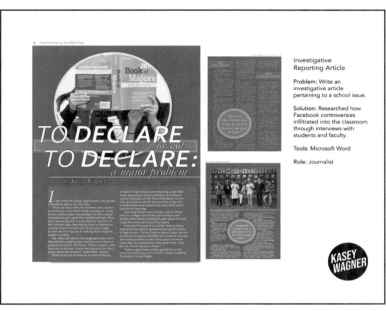

FIGURE 6-5 Showcasing written work.

PDF Conversion
You can make any Microsoft Word document a PDF file on a MAC or by using Adobe Acrobat on a Windows computer. Once you create the PDF, you can place it into other programs such as Microsoft Word, Adobe InDesign, or Google Docs. Remember, you won't beable to have fluid graphics in your online web portfolio with .PDF's, so you'll need to convert those files to .PNG or .JPG for placement in a website.

Have writing samples ready to go:
Be sure to carry along loose writing samples that you can leave with a hiring manager for further review. Choose a few writing samples to have ready. A short piece and a longer document if available (make them relevant). This is critical to have available if the job requires writing.

Showcasing visual work (still images and photographs)
Visual work is probably the easiest to represent in a portfolio, print or Web based because it is so literal and it is a single file to have to work with. The image is the image, which is viewed and then judged. Visual work can include any type of

image such as digital artwork and photographs. Artwork that is created on a computer, like a painting in Adobe Photoshop or a logo from Adobe Illustrator is already digitized and can be exported or saved out as a .JPG or .TIF file for placement into a portfolio layout. These images are easily placed in the portfolio layout. Work not in digital form includes fine artwork on paper or canvas, including pieces such as sketches, paintings, sculptures, installations, and drawings. These works need to be photographed or scanned to be placed into a portfolio. Paintings and drawings will scan and print well They should be captured at 300 dpi to final size for placement into the portfolio layout.

FIGURE 6-6 Showcasing visual work as digital and photographs requires a generous amount of space for content.

Showcasing data and presentations

Placing presentation materials in the print portfolio book can be valuable because many professional positions require presentations and showing ones that you have created shows you have experience. Putting data and presentations can be performed in a few ways. It depends on the slides, your role, and your goals. If the slides are visually stunning (and you designed them), you may want to show one slide larger with a few smaller slides. If the slides were part of a group project that you were part of with regards to content, you may want to show the slides in sequence smaller and then explain your role in the process. If you have a very longer slide show (more than 8-10 slides), you may want to present a few slides then place a caption that guides the reader to the full slide show online at your Web portfolio or "full presentation slides available upon request".

FIGURE 6-7 Showcasing research and presentation work can be done effectively with a case study. What is on the slide is not important at this point, the problem you attempted solve is what needs to be communicated.

Showcasing motion and web work
Motion and time based work needs to planned out so that it can be shown in a clear way using only two dimensions on paper. This can be achieved by showing key frames, which are instances where changes occur in animation, video, or any time-based work. Here are some types of visual work that can be shown in a key frame format:
> 2d and 3d Animations
> Banner ads
> Videos
> Television Commercials

Social posts
For motion work or social sequences, take multiple screenshots for each moment when there is a major change in action on the screen. Then, make sure that you crop and resize each image to the same dimensions. This will provide a uniform

appearance for your layout. Be sure to provide a case study or caption and include your role in the project (designer, writer, audio, etc.). You can present screenshots of single or multiple web pages to show online sites and banners.

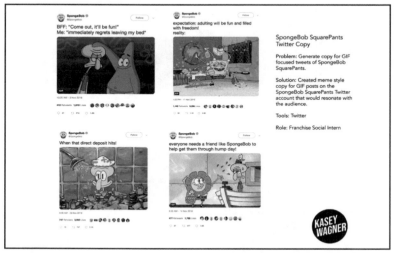

FIGURE 6-8 Showcasing motion, social, and web materials can be done with screenshots of key frames and important posts.

Explaining work

Explaining work is important in the portfolio. Because the print portfolio acts like a silent salesperson for your skills and abilities, it's important that you have clear definitions of your work. Just like photos and other images in a magazine or book, your work needs some item that explains it. The way you explain work is by writing captions or case studies.

Writing captions

Captions are the easier of the two. A caption is essentially a description of an image or work that provides uniform categories for each piece represented. Captions work great for images, but can also be written for other types of work.

Caption examples

ARTWORK:
Title: Self Portrait
Media: Pencil sketch
Year: 2012

CORPORATE PROJECT:
Project: Special Event Brochure
Programs: Adobe Photoshop, Adobe Indesign
Client: XCorp, Inc., 2012
Role: Copywriter and graphic designer

The caption can literally be anything you want it to be. It can be one line, two lines, three or four. It can have dates, or not. The only important requirement is that the caption be grammatically correct, accurate, and consistent throughout each section. Different sections may require different captions. That's okay, but make sure that you keep each set to the same number of lines. Otherwise, it could require you to adapt your layout due to less space, which will hurt the overall consistency of the portfolio book.

Writing case studies

Often it's not enough to simply write a caption for a piece of work. Some work is complicated in nature and needs further explanation. Or, the work may be industry specific and require extended breakdown of the goal of the project, what you did, and what was accomplished. That's essentially what the portfolio case study does; it presents a piece of work and provides a short summary of essential items such as what was the PROBLEM or GOAL, what was the SOLUTION or PROCESS, and what was the DELIVERABLE and YOUR ROLE. You can adapt this any way you like, but again make sure to keep it consistent across project sections.

Project case study example

PROBLEM: The non-profit student group, Hooper's Helpers needed to accumulate over 500 toys for the annual Toys-for-Tots toy drive

SOLUTION: In class, with a team of seven, built a campus-wide grassroots public relations campaign encouraging toy donations. Facilitated 10 collection box sites on campus. Over 1000 toys were donated during the campaign.

DELIVERABLES: A press release was written and distributed to local news outlets in NY City area. A social media campaign was developed and monitored using Facebook and Twitter pages.

ROLE: I performed writing and media relations for the project.

Technical project for a Corporation

PROJECT NAME:
CANON C3220 Color in the Office
Web Based Training Site. (WBT)

GOAL:
The goal of this project was to create an e-learning course that taught Canon dealers about the ImageRunner C3220 along with strategies for selling color in the office.

PROCESS:
Product specification documents and engineer's reports were used to extract critical talking points about the ImageRunner device and exclusive product features. The design integrated both html pages and web video portals.

ROLE:
I performed technical writing, conceptualization, design, and web programming for the entire website.

Case studies can be expanded upon and have up to 1-2 paragraphs per item. Any more becomes cumbersome to read, so keep it concise and clear. Case studies work well for professional written work such as press releases, ad copy, reports, presentations, white papers, journal articles, and books. They also are good for explaining academic work such as essays and team projects. You can include the case study on the page before the work to highlight it. Make sure that the case studies are written in the past tense. It's okay to use first person with "I".

EXERCISE (6F) - WRITE THE CAPTIONS OR CASE STUDIES
Begin to write the captions or cases and edit for spelling, grammar, and consistency. Each caption should be approximately the same length as the next.

Adding the personal logo

You should brand your print and Web portfolios with a personal logo. The personal logo adds graphic style to your portfolio book and Web portfolio. Be mindful of the font used, the color, and the size. Personal logos should not be larger than 1-2 inches in size. Ideally, you should be able to see the text clearly at 1 inch by 1 inch.
You can make a personal logo in the page layout program you will be using (such as MS Word or Adobe Indesign) or in an image editing application like Adobe Photoshop or an online DIY graphics editor like Canva.

Insert your personal logo just as you would an image into MS Word, Google Docs, or Adobe InDesign. Then, position the image in the same position on each page for a consistent, unified look.

FIGURE 6-9 Personal logo examples.

EXERCISE (6F) - CREATE A PERSONAL LOGO
Use Canva, Adobe Photoshop, or Illustrator to create a personal logo that promotes your personal brand.
REMEMBER! -- Save your logo as a 300 ppi graphic for your portfolio book and 72 ppi for your web portfolio. .PNG format with transparency works best for
both uses.

Editing and revision

You want to have someone else proof read your portfolio book. There are a few reasons for this. First, you need fresh eye to evaluate your pages and help find errors. Errors tend to blend in to pages when we look at something too long. Second, you want to avoid what I call "the proud proofer syndrome", which is when you are so proud of your work and what you created that you completely miss the mistakes.

These two cases happen to everyone so that's why we have proofreaders and editors. Find a friend, teacher, professor, advisor, mentor, former boss, or sibling that has a good command of English (or whichever language your book is in) and have them look over each page carefully. Print a copy for them and give them a red pen. Ask them to make comments, corrections, and suggestions. Make the changes that you feel are worthy.

Next, have someone else look it over and do the same thing. After you get two sets of eyes and have made changes, then print out your final book and have it bound. If you find an error after it's bound then reprint the offending page and bring the book back to where it was bound. The service provider should be able to unbind it, extract and replace the bad page and then rebind it.

Portfolio book finishing

This is where you finalize the portfolio design and finishing with a creative cover and useful binding. Beware, you need to keep it simple and try to make the cover eye-catching, but not overwhelming (unless that is the goal). Use your personal logo and maybe a short professional description of what you do...Something like Content Creator, or Marketing Professional, or whatever title fits your position...Something clear such as Teacher or Influencer.

The cover can include any of the following items:
- Your name
- Your personal logo
- Your title (Marketing Specialist or Graphic Designer or Biologist)
- A descriptive word or phrase can also be added ("professional portfolio" or "collection of works")
- One relevant, super crisp image

Binding the portfolio book

Binding can be spiral, comb, or anything you desire. The binding of the portfolio book serves two purposes. First, it holds the book together and second it adds a level of professional finishing to the project. Each binding has a slightly different cost. You can find out exact pricing at a local print shop or Staples.

I prefer the spiral, over the comb binding. The spiral is neater and holds the pages better. You can also create a custom binding with string or clasps, but be careful as the binding needs to be functional and strong enough to withstand use of the book. Binding can go on the short or long sides of the book. You can decide on binding when you complete the book, but you must remember to leave yourself the required 1.5 inch margin on the side of the page where the binding will be placed.

FIGURE 6-10 Print portfolio binding options.

You can also have separation pages that identify each section or opening pages that have a short case study written about the next page of work. These separator or entry pages can be on different paper, such as vellum or linen, which will add texture and elevate the visual style of the book.

FIGURE 6-11 Separator pages printed on vellum paper.

Creating the e-portfolio (PDF)

Once completed, you can output your print portfolio as a PDF file in either a Google app, Adobe, or Microsoft program as an e-portfolio, so that it can be emailed to a hiring manager or uploaded and linked to a Website.

This is the portfolio as a single, standalone electronic file with multiple pages that can be viewed in a Web browser or through Adobe Acrobat as a .PDF. This is different from a Web portfolio, which presents work on a series of Web pages on the Internet.

In Google Docs or MS. Word or PowerPoint: use the SAVE AS .PDF command or use the EXPORT FILE as .PDF.

Top five portfolio book errors to avoid

1. **Blurry, low resolution images** or text

2. **Spelling errors and grammar errors** in captions, cases, and samples

3. **Inconsistent placement of structure items:** headings, work sample, captions, and personal logos

4. **Images or text going into the binding** or off the page (without wanting a page bleed)

5. **Weak binding or sloppy cover**

Next chapter: Web portfolio
You are now into the final phase of building the ultimate set of career communication documents. So far we have walked through career planning, resume development, cover letter writing, and the design of a print portfolio book. These skills provide a host of tools for empowerment to find your next career and happiness opportunity. The career communication learning journey is almost complete. Finally, we compile what we have done so far and move on to designing the online Web portfolio.

Notes

Chapter 7.
WEB PORTFOLIO
Create your online brand.

Chapter objectives
- Understand the purpose of the Web portfolio
- Create a portfolio content list and site outline
- Gather and format your portfolio content
- Understand the style, length and design of the Web portfolio

Web portfolio overview
A web portfolio serves as a self selected, self developed, multimedia presentation of work that offers multiple views of a person's learning, professional and personal development throughout their life. It is a tool for presenting your skills and experience through a website.

You place your creative work, course work, personal work, and career work in your web portfolio. You gather up your work, both digital and hard copy, and place it in the pages of web portfolio. You write text in the portfolio that describes your skills, experience, goals, dreams, and personal value to society.

FIGURE 7-1 Web portfolios offer an online presentation tool beyond social media.

Google Tools for Web Portfolios

You can use a DIY website maker, as there are many, some free and some require a subscription. These include WIX, Weebly, SquareSpace, Google Sites, and WordPress.

I show my students how to use the FREE Google tool for websites, named Google Sites. To use google sites all you need is a Gmail account (which is a free Google account. Google Sites provides free Website design tools and hosting and supports all types of web portfolio and website designs including student, teacher/professor, company, career, and personal. There is no need to code to make a website, but if you do, you can enhance your Google site with HTML tags.

Web portfolios made with Google allow a wealth of analytic tools and search engine optimization tricks. They provide a dynamic platform for your career pitches and back your personal brand with real evidence. Web portfolios can be used across disciplines and majors. There are several types of Web portfolios which include:

Student Web portfolios

Student web portfolios show work from classes, volunteer work, and internship work. Use the web portfolio URL on your resume to show your professional identity. Use your portfolio for any course with a "portfolio requirement", including graphic design, education, communications, management, computer science, humanities, and natural sciences. People across disciplines can utilize web portfolios.

Career Web portfolios

Career web portfolios are for job seekers and graduates who are trying to get ahead in their professions. Regardless of the field or industry, everyone has accomplishments that they need to share with potential employers. Web portfolios are great for presenting your experience beyond the resume. They put you ahead of the competition. Many companies in the creative and teaching fields demand an online portfolio for job candidates. We demonstrate the career portfolio in this chapter.

Teacher/Professor Web portfolios

These web portfolios can be used to show professional

development work, student work, creative projects, scholarly papers, syllabi's, and course lessons. The web portfolio provides evidence of lifelong learning and is slowly becoming a standard tool for tenure/promotion and assessment practices.

Company Web portfolios
Company web portfolios provide evidence of the products, services, and expertise possessed by a company. Freelancers, consultants, designers, and all small businesses need a website that promotes their talents, and showcases products and projects.

Personal Web portfolios:
Personal portfolios are for everyone. They can present photos, videos, artwork, writing, and design. They provide a creative place for posting your personal work about hobbies, groups, fan followings, family, and friends.

Why use a Web portfolio?
- A web portfolio provides tangible evidence of your skills and experience.

- A web portfolio sets you apart from other applicants who don't have one.

- A web portfolio allows you to connect with your own work and will help you talk about it in an interview.

- A web portfolio gives you confidence because it is a self promotional tool that can do the talking for you.

- A web portfolio expands beyond the print portfolio to show a larger field of live work samples.

- A web portfolio can be updated quickly, easily, and regularly.

- A web portfolio allows people to find you and your work on the Web.

- A web portfolio can be used as a freelance or business Website.

- Building a web portfolio is the highest level of cognitive learning objective - creating. When you create a web portfolio, you are learning.

How to create a web portfolio

Creating a web portfolio includes a series of steps:
1. Reflect and collect work
2. Prepare work for the web
3. Build and publish your site to the web

Reflect, collect, and plan

Reflect - define your role in the professional world

First, complete this statement: My Web portfolio promotes me as a _____.

Now place the most relevant content into your Web portfolio that supports that sentence. You can ultimately put in everything that you have ever done into the Web portfolio. This gives you a personal archive. But for now, just put in the best, most important items. Then, you can expand on the web portfolio and add to it as your skills and experience increase.

Collect - What can go in the Web portfolio

It depends on your area of expertise. Some jobs require certain work samples, so refer back to your jobs and skills research. You will need to reflect on what you have done in the past and collect the work (artifacts).

Here are some basic suggestions for the items to put in the web portfolio:
• Personal photo
• Project samples
• Writing samples
• Blogs and Vlogs
• Social media page links
• Student project work
• Art and design work
• Photos
• Professional activities
• Presentations
• Events

- Volunteer work
- Project case studies
- Animations (share from YouTube)
- Video clips (share from YouTube)
- Illustrations
- Digital Images
- Professional Goals
- Personal Mission Quote
- Research reports/papers
- Lesson plans (teachers)

Write the content list

The content list is a list of all the materials that you would like to put in the Web portfolio in no particular order. The main goal here is to be specific in your descriptions of work so that you can identify the file during production and presentation. And second, which is the most important part of this process, is to be able to collect a sample of the work in digital form. You need digital files as .JPG or .PNG for the website. You may need to shoot a picture or scan a hard copy to get work into digital form. Without the digital file, you can't put the work into the Website. If this is not possible you should cross the work off the laundry list.

Sample content List of work:

- **Lego ad - class project**
- **Environment essay**
- **WWII history animation project**
- **Photos of sunsets**
- **Video for charity sports event**
- **Still life painting of fruit**
- **Drawing series - human form**

EXERCISE (7A): WEB PORTFOLIO CONTENT LIST
Write a list of potential work for the web portfolio (be specific in naming - for example: "Italian landscape photo" or "food drive volunteer photo -2010". You can start with the list from your print portfolio and add other web based work samples.

Create the flow chart

The content outline is a list of all the materials that you would like to put in the Web portfolio in order with the appropriate navigation headings. It marries the "sections" with the "samples". The content outline can be drawn as a flowchart so that you can get a sense of the visual flow of the Website.

This is where you establish your Website navigation & sections and add projects from the laundry list you created earlier. Navigation sections should consist of major areas that you have sample work for. These can be broad categories such as "writing", which could have a variety of writing samples, or they can be a narrow category like "press releases". It depends on how many pieces you have and what the industry is that you are promoting yourself in is looking for. Look to the keywords you researched to get some suggested headings. For navigation, you will be able to place subheads (sub navigation) for sections (navigation) if you like. This means that a navigation section might be titled "Projects", then underneath is sub navigation to the individual projects "Non-profit brochure", for example. This structure allows you to organize the work clearly and then have a direct path to add work in each navigation section or add a new section.

EXERCISE (7B): CREATE THE CONTENT OUTLINE
DEVELOP THE WEB PORTFOLIO NAVIGATION SECTIONS. LIST THE NAVIGATION HEADINGS AND THEN ADD THE CONTENT FROM THE CONTENT LIST UNDER THE APPROPRIATE SECTIONS. BE SPECIFIC IN NAMING THE CONTENT.

You might think of other work that you have not yet completed but plan to put into the portfolio in the future (as in the case of working on this during a school semester). You can leave a placeholder page in the website and make that page "hidden" until you have completed the work and placed it in the Web page.

To make the flowchart, simply create lines that connect boxes and other lines. The boxes will represent pages and page links and the information on the lines will represent the content.

EXERCISE (7C): CREATE THE FLOW CHART
Place the sections and lower content from the outline into a flow chart, which will show the basic flow of the website from page to page.

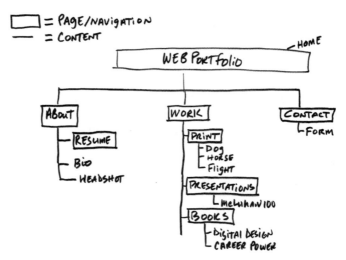

FIGURE 7-2 Content outline and flowchart sample

Prepare digital work

There are several kinds of content formats that you will use to show work in your Web portfolio: text, images, video, audio, and animations. Text based work can be copied and pasted or typed directly into a DIY website maker such as Google sites. Images will need to be inserted into the Web page alongside text.

Web portfolios are output on a screen, so the resolution of images that go on the pages does not have to be over 72 dpi to size. If you scan images, 96 dpi to size is a good target resolution for images that will be uploaded and placed into Web pages. Use low resolution settings on your digital camera if you are taking photos of work or events that will be published on the Web portfolio site. This will insure the most economical size for the images

All images need to be RGB color or Index color. CMYK files won't work in Web pages. As far as formats, You can use .JPG or .PNG for images. The PNG file format will preserve transparency on images so that they can be laid over other images or color and have no outline or white box background. Image you are standing in front of a blue wall and we take a photo of you and open it on a computer. Using Adobe Photoshop or any other image editing program, you can select the blue wall and delete it out, leaving a transparent background (checkerboard). In PNG format you will be cut out and the background will be gone. In .JPG Format, you will have a white background to the boundaries of the image.

Converting Hi-Res images for print to Low Res images for the web
You can convert your high resolution .TIF or .JPG images into low resolution .JPG or PNG images for placement into your Website by opening them in Adobe Photoshop and selecting the menu item > IMAGE > IMAGE SIZE, then, type in 72 in the resolution. Keep the file size and dimensions the same and make sure that the file is RGB color mode, 8 bit (IMAGE > COLOR MODE) - If it isn't RGB, click RGB in the menu to convert it.

If you use screenshots of your work, they can go directly into Web pages as they are low resolution (96 or 72 dpi). They will look crisp and clean on the Web pages as long as they are not scaled much larger than the original.

If you haven't already, create two folders: "HIGH RES-PRINT" and "LOW RES-WEB". Copy all the files from the HIGH RES folder into the LOW RES folder.

Convert and resize any images that are too large or need file format conversions to .JPG or .PNG for web. Then when you begin to create your site, you will upload the images and files you need from the low res folder into the file manager of the website maker.

Converting PowerPoint presentations to .JPG files.
You can easily convert PowerPoint presentations by going to SAVE AS and dropping down to .JPG or using the SAVE AS IMAGES command. Then confirm that you want all slides and you will get a .JPG for each slide that can be arranged on a Web page, or in a slide show gallery.

Build and publish your web portfolio

You will use Google sites to create your web portfolio. If you want to use another tool, that is okay, the import thing is that you add pages and content in a clear structure. You should have your files located in one folder from before – DRAG that folder on to your Google drive for easy placements.

1. Setup Your Free Google Account.

You'll need to have a Google account to use Google sites. Create one at Google.com for free.

2. Launch Google Drive to access tools

Go to www.Google.com and click on the menu next to your name and click DRIVE

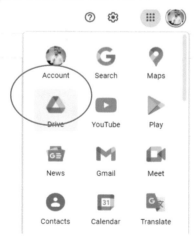

3. Create a new site
Select the + and MORE, then click > GOOGLE SITES.

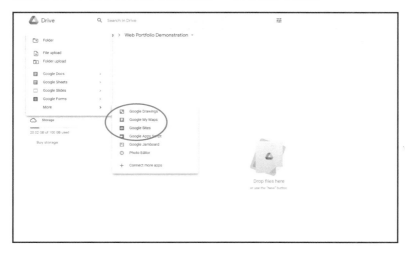

4. Create pages and sub pages
Click > PAGES use the + to add pages.

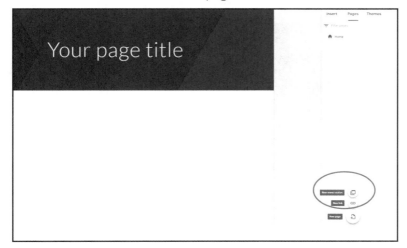

Use the : menu next to the pages to add subpages.

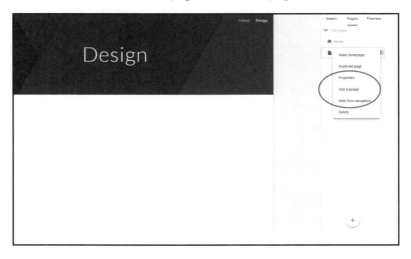

5. Set up your Page Master
Add a logo and favicon. Click the Add logo button to insert the logo and favicon into the web page header.

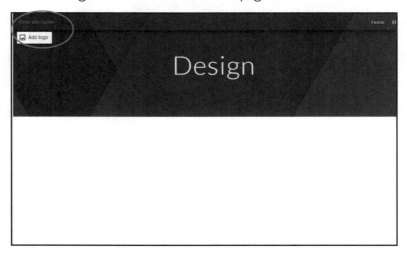

6. Add page headers to each page

You can delete the existing header at the page top and add a more dynamic graphic (roll over the left side of panel and click the trash can to delete.) To add a new header, scroll over the heading area at the top of the page. You can set it as a banner, cover, or title only.

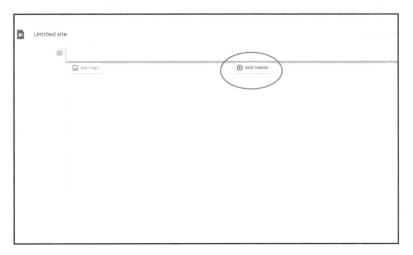

7. Add content

From the INSERT Menu - Add text, Images, and Video - Adjust the layout and fonts. This is a cover header graphic.

8. Build interactivity into the Web Portfolio

Add links to URLS, web site pages, and social feeds.

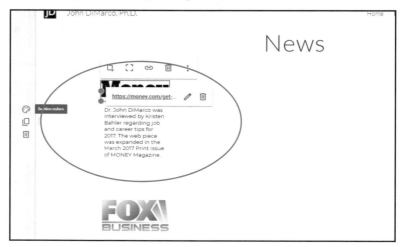

9. Publish your website

Set up your website address to the standard Google subdirectory address or your own URL.

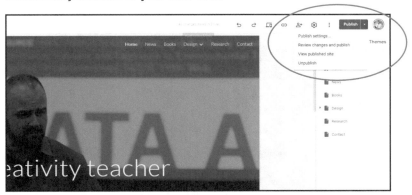

10. Review your site for errors and missing links

Click through the entire site to insure that every button, menu, and link is working properly. Sample site pages below made by the author using Google Sites.

Bio and header image on homepage.

News page with external links.

Books page with text, graphics and external links.

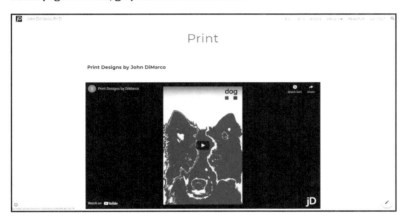

Design page with YouTube video of work.

Notes

BIBLIOGRAPHY

Baker, W. H., DeTienne, K., & Smart, K. L. (1998). How Fortune 500 Companies Are Using Electronic Résumé Management Systems. Business Communication Quarterly, 61(3), 8–19. https://doi. org/10.1177/108056999806100302

Cenedella, M. (2020). How to write the best résumé for 2020. Retrieved 4 January 2020, from https://www.fastcompany. com/90446884/how-to-write-thebest-resume-for-2020

Chowdhury, A. (2020). The New Science Of Resumes–And Why Yours Sinks To The Bottom Of The Pile. Retrieved 4 January 2020, from https://www. fastcompany.com/3002273/new-science-resumes-and-why-yours-sinks-bottompile

Controller, C. (2020, January 2). Medical Benefits and Health Insurance. In Complete Controller. Retrieved from https://www.completecontroller.com/medical-benefits-and-health-insurance/

Creswell, J., & Creswell, J. Research design (6th ed., pp. 86-87). Los Angeles: Sage.

Culwell-Block, B., and Sellers, J. A. (1994). Resume content and format - do the authorities agree? The Bulletin of the Association for Business Communication, 57(4), p.27. Retrieved from http://jerome.stjohns.edu:81/login?url=https:// search-proquest-com.jerome.stjohns.edu/docview/236870932?accountid=14068

Diaz, C. (2013). Updating Best Practices: Applying on-screen reading strategies to resume writing. Business Communication Quarterly, 76(4), 427-445. doi: 10.1177/1080569913501860

DiMarco, J. (2013) Career Power Skills. Boston: Pearson.

DiMarco, J. and Fasos, S. (2019), Resume content research across disciplines: an analysis of ProQuest from 1984-2018, The Electronic Library. https://doi.org/10.1108/EL-07-2019-0175

Doyle, A. (2020, July 21). Vacation Time and Pay For Employees. In The Balance Careers. Retrieved from https://www.thebalancecareers.com/how-much-vacation-time-and-pay-do-employees-get-2064018#:~:text=There%20isn

Eye Tracking Study 2018 - The Ladders. (2020). Retrieved from http:// go.theladders.com/rs/539-NBG-120/images/EyeTracking-Study.pdf

Harcourt, J., and Others, A. (1991). Teaching resume content: Hiring officials' preferences versus college recruiters' preferences. Business Education Forum, 45(7), pp.13-17. Retrieved from http://jerome.stjohns.edu:81/login?url=https:// search-proquest- com.jerome.stjohns.edu/docview/63003692?accountid=14068

Hiemstra, A. M. F., Derous, E., Serlie, A. W., and Born, M. P. (2013). Ethnicity effects in graduates' résumé content. Applied Psychology, 62(3), pp.427-453. doi:http://dx.doi.org.jerome.stjohns.edu:81/10.1111/j.1464-0597.2012.00487.x

Hornsby, J. S., and Smith, B. N. (1995). Resume content: What should be included and excluded. S.A.M.Advanced Management Journal, 60(1), 4. Retrieved from http://jerome.stjohns.edu:81/login?url=https://search-proquestcom.jerome.stjohns.edu/docview/231245920?accountid=14068

Lo, M. (n.d.). How to contribute more at the workplace. In The Nest. Retrieved from https://woman.thenest.com/contribute-workplace-11213.html

Nielsen, J. (2020). F-Shaped Pattern of Reading on the Web: Misunderstood, But Still Relevant (Even on Mobile). Retrieved 17 January 2020, from https://www.nngroup.com/articles/f-shaped-pattern-reading-web-content/

Schramm, R. M., and Dortch, R. N. (1991). An analysis of effective resume content, format, and appearance based on college recruiter perceptions. Bulletin of the Association for Business Communication, 54(3), pp.18-23. Retrieved from http://jerome.stjohns.edu:81/login?url=https://search-proquest- com.jerome.stjohns.edu/docview/62903159?accountid=14068

Stephens, D., Watt, J., & Hobbs, W. (1979). Getting Through the Resume Preparation Maze: Some Empirically Based Guidelines for Resume Format. Vocational Guidance Quarterly, 28(1), 25-34. doi: 10.1002/j.2164-585x.1979. Tb00080.x

Shrestha, S., Owens, J., & Chaparro, B. (2008). Eye Movements on a SingleColumn and Double-Column Text Web Page. Proceedings Of The Human Factors And Ergonomics Society Annual Meeting, 52(19), 1599-1603. doi: 10.1177/154193120805201962

Tsai, W., Chi, N., Huang, T., & Hsu, A. (2011). The effects of applicant resume contents on recruiters' hiring recommendations: The mediating roles of recruiter fit perceptions. Applied Psychology: An International Review, 60(2), 231-254.

Weeg, B. E. (1992). An evaluation of the resume content recommendations of resume writing books. Reference Librarian, (36), pp.153-171. Retrieved from http://jerome. stjohns.edu:81/login?url=https://search-proquest- com. jerome. stjohns.edu/docview/57309109?accountid=14068

Wilson, M. (2020). How To Redesign Your Resume For A Recruiter's 6-Second Attention Span. Retrieved from https:// www.fastcompany.com/1669531/howto-redesign-your- resume-for-a-recruiter-s-6-second-attention-span

Womack, K., and Goldberg, T. (1997). Resume content: Applicants' perceptions. College and Research Libraries, 58(6), pp.540-549. Retrieved from http:// jerome.stjohns. edu:81/login?url=https://search-proquest- com.jerome. stjohns. edu/docview/57433514?accountid=14068

Zhang, L. (n.d.). Everything you need to know about internships - From what they are to how to get one. In The Muse. Retrieved from https://www.themuse.com/ advice/what-is-an-internship-definition-advice

Resources

Getting access to resume, cover letter, and portfolio templates
1. Go to www.portfoliovillage.com and set up your free account.
2. Once you have your account, download the template documents to your computer (resume, cover letter, reference sheet, and portfolio books)
3. Read each chapter of this book, take notes in the text, and use the templates to create the documents. You can refer to the text and free video lessons and lectures at www.portfoliovillage.com.
4. Access the Google sites reference materials at portfoliovillage.com to create your web portfolio.

Scan to access portfoliovillage.com for templates, video lectures from Dr. DiMarco and step by step lessons.

Index

About the author

John DiMarco, Ph.D. has been helping people and organizations with design and communication for 25 years. He teaches undergraduate and continuing education courses on career skills, writing, digital design, and advertising. His ability to transfer skills and creative process make him a sought after professor, coach, and mentor in design, communication, career skills, and entrepreneurship.

Dr. DiMarco has authored five books with Wiley, Pearson, Wiley Blackwell and IGI. As well, he has published dozens of articles and chapters in academic textbooks and peer-reviewed journals.

A designer by trade and practice, John DiMarco holds a United States Patent and Trademark for his invention Shape Stretch, a revolutionary body stretching bar and flexibility education system. He holds a Ph,D. in Information Studies, is an Adobe Education Trainer, and a NASM Certified Stretching and Flexibility Coach.

Connect with John on LinkedIn at:
https://www.linkedin.com/in/drjohndimarco/

Other books by John DiMarco
DiMarco, J. 2017. Communications Writing and Design: An Integrated Manual for Marketing, Advertising, and Public Relations. Hoboken: Wiley Blackwell, John Wiley & Sons. Includes Instructor decks, quizzes, PDF's, and learning videos.

DiMarco, J. 2013. Career Power Skills: The Simple Guide to Researching Careers and Creating your Resume, Cover letter, Print Portfolio, E-Portfolio, and Online Web Portfolio. New York: Pearson Education. OUT OF PRINT

DiMarco, J. 2010. Digital Design for Print and Web: An Introduction to Theory, Principles, and Techniques. Hoboken: John Wiley and Sons.

DiMarco, J. 2006. Web Portfolio Design and Applications. Hershey: Idea-Group.

DiMarco, J. (Ed) 2004. Computer Graphics and Multimedia: Applications, Problems, and Solutions. Hershey: Idea-Group.

Made in the USA
Columbia, SC
05 August 2024

40043489R00096